Past-into-Present Series

Universities

D. J. Thomas

Head of Commerce, Churchfields High School, West Bromwich

B. T. BATSFORD LTD   London

For Stephanie and Helen

First published 1973
© D. J. Thomas 1973

Filmset by Keyspools Ltd, Golborne, Lancs.

Printed in Great Britain by The Anchor Press Ltd, Tiptree, Essex
for the Publishers
B. T. Batsford Ltd, 4 Fitzhardinge Street, London W1V OAH

ISBN 0 7134 1783 8

Contents

Acknowledgment

The author would like to thank Miss M. S. Lawrence for her helpful suggestions and for typing the manuscript. The author and publishers are grateful for the co-operation of many universities in the collecting of pictures and would particularly like to thank the following for the illustrations which appear in this book: Aerofilms Ltd for fig. 16; Angus McBean and the Oxford Playhouse for fig 57; the University of Aston in Birmingham for figs, 38, 40, 46 and 65; the University of Bath for figs. 37 and 41; the Bodlean Library, Oxford, for fig. 44; the British Museum for fig. 14; St David's College, Lampeter, for fig. 34; the University of Dundee for figs 29 and 30; the University of Exeter for fig 52; *Glasgow Herald* for fig. 48; the University of Keele for fig. 25; the Mansell Collection for figs. 2, 3, 9, 10, 11, 15, 17, 19, 21, 23, 27, 28, 32, 50, 51, 55, and 56; the *Midland Bank Review* for fig. 35; the University of Newcastle for fig. 42; the Open University for figs. 59–64; Oxford City Library for fig. 39; Oxford University Press for fig. 58; Radio Times Hulton Picture Library for figs. 18, 20 and 31; the University of Salford for fig. 43; the University of Sheffield and Firth and Brown Ltd for fig. 22; the University of Sussex for fig. 45.

The Illustrations

1 Oxford and Cambridge

Medieval Origins

The origins of universities lie in the Middle Ages. Nothing really corresponding to the modern university can be found in Ancient Greece or Rome. Groups of scholars might have gathered round famous teachers, but they do not seem ever to have created a continuing organisation. The disintegration of the ancient world reduced scholarly life to a low level, but by the twelfth century, that life was being renewed in a remarkable era which historians call the *Renaissance*.

It is not possible to give a precise date for the origin of universities, but in the early twelfth century, long before universities were organised as such, students were gathering together for higher studies at certain definite centres. Paris was frequented especially for philosophy and theology; Bologna for law and Salerno for medicine. Each of these centres was known as a *studium generale*, that is, a place of learning open to students from all lands.

Dr Rashdall, who made a study of the medieval universities, confidently asserted that the establishment of a *studium generale* at Oxford could be pinpointed to a migration from Paris in the year 1167. Other historians consider there is little evidence to support this assertion. There is, however, clear evidence that a *studium generale* existed at Oxford about 1185.

But why at Oxford?

It was an important town long before the university appeared. Its river crossings (hence Oxen-ford) made it an important frontier position between the Saxon

1 Students at Bologna. The word *universitas*, meaning 'a whole', was originally used to describe an association of students, although this was not an organised university as we know it. Students from many countries collected at the main centres such as Bologna and Paris and often grouped themselves into schools or 'nations'. Travelling was dangerous and wars sometimes disrupted teaching. Such difficulties contributed to migration of students to new centres.

kingdoms of Wessex and Mercia. Oxford was highly favoured by both Henry I and Henry II. The former built a palace and kept a hunting lodge close to the town while the latter gave to the citizens a charter granting certain privileges. Thus geographical position and royal favour together with commercial prosperity (a wealthy community of Jews flourished under royal protection) probably explain the growth of a *studium generale* at Oxford.

Cambridge University originated as the result of a migration of scholars from Oxford in 1209. The cause of the migration was a quarrel between the scholars and citizens of Oxford. A student killed an Oxford woman and fled for his life. The mayor and burgesses marched to the fugitive's lodgings and failing to find him, carried off three of his fellow students and hanged them. In protest, the university dispersed to other towns, Cambridge among them. Not until five years later did the citizens of Oxford make their peace with the Oxford scholars. All those who had been involved in the hangings were required to do penance and students living in the town were granted reductions in the rents charged for their lodgings.

It is not known why some of the Oxford students selected Cambridge but the migration assisted in the development of a new *studium generale* at that town.

Development of the Colleges

In their early days, neither Oxford nor Cambridge owned buildings and students were left to find their own lodgings. However, the custom developed of groups of students renting houses for themselves and electing one of their number to be responsible for the rest. Gradually these hostels or Halls came under the control of the university with the elected representative (or Principal) responsible for payment of the rent and the discipline of the boarders.

To support poor students, endowed hostels were set up by wealthy benefactors. Some of these endowed houses for poor scholars developed into the present-day

2 Seal of Sir John de Balliol.

colleges. In the middle of the thirteenth century, William of Durham endowed a house at Oxford known as Great University Hall, which became, about 1280, University College. The House of Balliol was founded as a penance for his sins by Sir John de Balliol. This foundation developed into Balliol College. In 1264 Walter de Merton, Chancellor of England founded the 'House of the Scholars of Merton'. At Cambridge a similar development took place and Hugh de Balsham, the Bishop of Ely endowed 'The House of Peter' which became Peterhouse College.

The Medieval Curriculum

How did the medieval student entering the university at the age of 14 or 15, fill his days? As an undergraduate he studied for three years before presenting himself for the degree of Bachelor. The course he studied was based upon the seven liberal arts, divided into the trivium of grammar, rhetoric and logic, and the quadrivium of geometry, arithmetic, astronomy and music.

The teaching method of the universities took two forms, namely, that of the *lectio* and that of the *quaestio*. The *lectio* took the form of the reading and explanation of a

3 The reading of the Foundation Charter of King's College, Cambridge. Very often, the founder of a college drew up regulations for the corporate life of the fellows. Some statutes ordered, for example, that those under the age of 18 who missed a chapel attendance were to be publicly birched; those over 18 were to be fined.

textbook. The lecturer read the text paragraph by paragraph, and at the end of each one commented to his audience on its content. Some lecturers read quickly while others spoke at a pace which was slow enough for students to write down both the dictated text and the lecturer's commentary. While the latter type of lecturer was, no doubt, popular with his students because they saved the cost of buying books, the sales of the booksellers suffered. Consequently some of the early regulations required the lecturer to read at a normal conversational pace!

The *quaestio* was an exercise in disputation between the lecturer and his students. Disputations were closely connected with topics arising out of the lectures and were a means of testing a student's knowledge of the set books.

The examination for the degree of Bachelor was in three parts. A preliminary test called *Responsions* involved a disputation in logic and grammar with a master. If he passed this successfully, the candidate appeared before a board of examiners who satisfied themselves that he had fulfilled the conditions of residence and attended the necessary lectures. They then proceeded to question him on the books he had studied. The final stage of the examination was the *Determination*. This took the form of a disputation in which the candidate determined (or provided) a solution of the problem he had chosen to dispute. The Determination took place before an audience comprising the masters and fellow students of the candidate. The general public were also able to attend.

Four more years of study and disputation were required before a Bachelor could

4 Medieval colleges such as Clare College, Cambridge (left), were not founded for undergraduates. They were designed for those taking the long and expensive training for the M.A. and the higher degrees of doctorates. The scholars who lived in the college were known as fellows. Only All Souls' College, Oxford, remains today as a college without undergraduates, but in the fourteenth century such a college was the rule rather than the exception.

proceed to the degree of Master of Arts. Another five or more years were required for the Doctorate and the rigorous and expensive training made this higher degree a highly valued prize.

Royal Protection

Oxford and Cambridge enjoyed the favour of both kings and popes – and for sound practical reasons. A supply of men with literate, trained minds was required for the administration of the Church and later, under Henry VIII, for the royal and national administration. Training for statesmen and civil servants was provided by the universities and there was real point to the bidding prayer at Oxford University sermons asking 'that there may never be wanting a succession of persons duly qualified for the service of God in Church and State'.

At the time of the Reformation the suppression of the monasteries aroused fears in the universities of a similar attack on the college endowments. The king, Henry VIII, was quick to offer reassurance: 'I judge no land in England better bestowed than that which is given to our Universities. For by their maintenance our Realm shall be well governed when we be dead and rotten'.

Social Change

In the sixteenth century a change took place in the type of student who entered the universities. The number of the 'poor scholars' of medieval times began to decline

5   A plan of Cambridge.

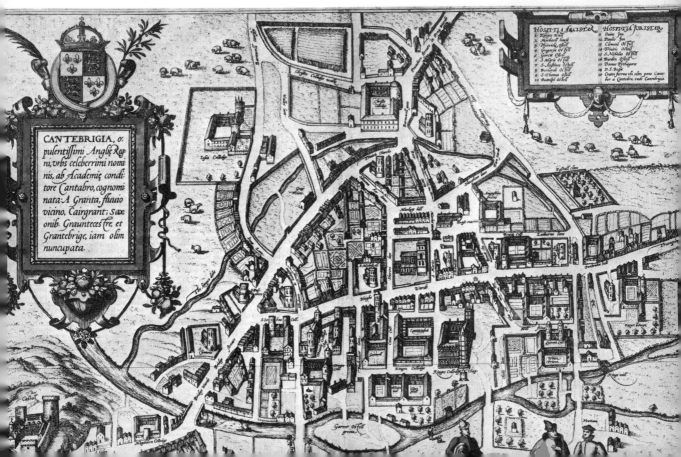

while the nobility and gentry moved into the universities in ever-increasing numbers. The system was developing by which the fellows of the colleges acted as private tutors to small groups of students. This new departure strengthened the quality of the teaching at the universities but it also resulted in tutors favouring richer students and neglecting the poorer ones. Bishop Latimer complained in 1549 that 'there be none now but great men's sons in colleges' but it seems likely that the reports of nobles and gentry monopolising the universities were exaggerated. Nonetheless there was a marked change in the social composition of university students.

There were two main reasons for the change.

In the first place the gentry had begun to appreciate the value of higher education as an aid to carrying out their duties as a governing class. Secondly, the humanist movement (a re-discovery of the values of the ancient world of Greece and Rome) had a strong influence in the universities in this century. It convinced the gentry that virtue, wisdom and good manners were to be obtained through higher education.

Thus a gentleman, especially if he aspired to serve the State, finished his education at a university. For example, Sir Philip Sidney and Sir Walter Raleigh were at Oxford; William Cecil and Sir Francis Bacon were at Cambridge.

Eighteenth-Century Decline

During the eighteenth century the two universities sank into a position which, to a large extent, made them a preserve for the idle and the rich. The university

6 Oxford in the mid-eighteenth century.

7 In the eighteenth century the universities had become places 'where great numbers were maintained who neither study themselves nor concern themselves in superintending the studies of others' (Vicesimus Knox). Those of noble birth wore caps with gold tassels and embroidered gowns.

colleges had, for the most part, been founded primarily for the benefit of poor students who received assistance from endowments. But by the eighteenth century there had grown up the practice of receiving large numbers of students who paid fees for tuition and maintenance. At Oxford these students were known as Commoners and the equivalent at Cambridge was the Pensioner. They greatly outnumbered the 'poor scholars'. Undergraduates of noble birth had the privilege of wearing an embroidered gown of purple silk and a college cap with a gold tassel. They were further distinguished by being entirely excused the examinations which led to a degree.

In any case examinations were farcical. The forms of the medieval disputations were still maintained but they were 'for the most part performed in so negligent a manner, that it is equally impossible that they should contribute to the advancement of learning, to the improvement of the candidate, or to the honour of the University'. So wrote Dr John Napleton, Vice-Principal of Brasenose College, Oxford in 1773. Another writer described how to complete his test for the degree, the candidate was obliged to present himself before the examiners to answer questions. 'If the Vice-Chancellor . . . happen to enter . . . a little solemnity is put on.' Otherwise 'the examiners and the candidates often converse on the last drinking bout, or on horses, or read the newspapers or a novel'.

The same author, Vicesimus Knox, wrote a startling account of the depths to which the universities had declined. 'Many of those houses which the piety and charity of the founders consecrated to religion, virtue, learning, everything useful and lovely, are become the seats of ignorance, infidelity, corruption, and debauchery.'

13

8 Although attempts were being made to reform the universities, this cartoon by Rowlandson, published in 1824, illustrates the contemporary view of university life.

Reform

Towards the end of the eighteenth century attempts were made to reform the curriculum and the tests for the degrees. Written examinations were added to the oral and in time, began to carry more weight than the old *viva-voce* tests.

Classics formed the chief characteristic of the Oxford course at this time, though some mathematics was included. In 1807 the classics and mathematics honours schools were divided. The honours schools soon began to win a high place in public esteem. It became possible for an exceptional candidate to gain a 'double first' (in classics and mathematics). In 1808 Peel was the first graduate with a double first and Gladstone took such a degree in 1831.

At Cambridge in 1824 a second Tripos was established in classics. The original had been in mathematics. The name 'Tripos' has a medieval origin. In the fifteenth century, according to S. C. Roberts, the gentleman who disputed with the candidates 'had sat on a three-legged stool and was known as "Mr Tripos". He had been in the habit of writing frivolous verses on the subject of disputation. These were known as "Tripos Verses" and survived long after the original Mr Tripos had gone. In 1747 the custom was begun of printing the candidates' names in order of merit on the back of the sheet of verses, and hence the name Tripos came to be applied to the examination itself'.

The widening of the curriculum is indicated by the institution at Cambridge during the eighteenth century of a number of new professorships, several of them in scientific subjects. By 1851 there were Triposes in moral science and natural science. By 1850 the Oxford honours schools included mathematics, natural science, law, modern history and theology.

The Oxford University Act of 1854 and the Cambridge University Act of 1856 removed religious tests for admission to the universities or for taking the degree of B.A. (Hitherto those who were not members of the Church of England had been unable to enter the university. Thus, for example, non-conformists, Jews, Roman Catholics and secularists had been excluded.) The test was not finally abolished for all degrees (except for those in divinity) until 1871.

A number of new professorships were founded and the professors were given a place of greater importance in university administration. Many professorships now had college fellowships attached to them, and this strengthened the link between the university and the colleges. These reforms brought new life and vigour to the universities. The number of undergraduates grew rapidly and in 1871 the distinctions between noblemen, gentlemen commoners, and commoners disappeared. New final honours schools or triposes were instituted in Oriental languages, English language and literature, and medieval and modern languages.

A further Act – the Oxford and Cambridge Act, 1877 – introduced more reforms

9 The higher education of women. An extract from the *Times*, 1877, showing, left to right, top: the portress and the terrace at Newnham Hall, and a lecture; centre: a study, Girton College; bottom: afternoon tea, the laboratory, and the dining hall, Girton College.

which, together with the earlier measures, transformed Oxford and Cambridge from a group of largely clerical institutions into modern universities. To this period belongs the founding of colleges and halls for women – Girton and Newnham at Cambridge, Somerville and Lady Margaret Hall at Oxford. Women were not however, admitted to full membership of the university at Oxford until 1920, and at Cambridge, until 1948.

Today, Oxford and Cambridge are the leading examples of collegiate universities in the modern world. The colleges are corporate bodies governed by their own fellows and distinct from the university. Most of the fellows of the colleges, however, are university teachers or officers and the majority of university teachers are also fellows of colleges.

FURTHER READING

T. L. Jarman, *Landmarks in the History of Education* Cresset Press
C. R. Benstead, *Portrait of Cambridge* Robert Hale
F. Markham, *Oxford* Weidenfeld and Nicolson
H. Rashdall, *The Universities of Europe in the Middle Ages* Oxford University Press

2 London

Origins

Plans for a university in London date from the sixteenth century, but the movement of opinion which brought the university into being dates from soon after 1820. This movement began with a letter written by Thomas Campbell, the poet, and printed in the *Times* on 9 February 1825. Campbell urged the establishment of a 'great London University' designed to educate the middle classes. The movement was supported by a group of influential dissenters, Whigs and Radicals which included Francis Place, Jeremy Bentham, Dr Birkbeck, Henry Brougham and Joseph Hume. A gathering of interested persons presided over by the Lord Mayor met at the London Tavern and a joint-stock company was formed called the Proprietors of the University of London. The company issued a prospectus and launched an appeal for funds. The aim was to found a college in London to give a broad and wholly non-sectarian education in arts, science and medicine. The money raised was used to purchase a site in Gower Street and the foundation stone of the new University was laid in 1827.

10 Thomas Campbell. In the early nineteenth century there had developed a large and dissatisfied opposition to the control of higher education by Oxford and Cambridge. There were three main criticisms. In the first place, the high cost of student life effectively barred most middle-class and working-class people. Secondly, admission was restricted to students who were members of the Church of England. The third factor was that the curricula of the Colleges paid little attention to scientific and technical subjects. Campbell, Brougham and Hume were leading members of the opposition.

In 1828 the first classes were held and the curriculum embraced languages, mathematics, physics, law, history, political economy and medicine. By 1830 over 500 students had been enrolled. The annual fees varied from £25 to £30 and were cheap because the University was non-residential. Several of the promoters had had experience of this kind of university organisation. Thomas Campbell had visited the non-residential universities in Germany and a number of his fellow supporters had been educated in Scottish universities which were run on similar lines. They were well aware, therefore, of the advantages of a non-residential university where cheap fees would give the middle classes access to higher education.

The constitution laid down that the University was to be an undenominational teaching institution; there were to be no religious tests for students and theology was excluded from the curriculum. The secular constitution aroused a great deal of opposition. Like Thomas Arnold, many Anglicans thought of the new university as 'that godless institution in Gower Street'. W. M. Praed described it as 'the radical infidel college'. Some dissenters, believing religion to be the basis of all

11 Cruikshank's cartoon, *The Political Toyman*. The aims of the promoters of London University—to provide cheap, non-sectarian literary and scientific education—drew a good deal of derisory comment.

stages of education, were also dismayed by the complete secularisation of the university. It is, perhaps, almost impossible for students today to imagine the extent to which religious thought pervaded education in the early nineteenth century.

The opposition was headed by the Rector of Lambeth, Dr George D'Oyley, who proposed the establishment of a rival institution in which religious instruction should form an essential part of the curriculum. A public meeting was held on 21 June 1828. The Prime Minister, the Duke of Wellington, was in the chair, and the Archbishops of Canterbury and York were among the clergy assembled on the platform. The meeting passed a resolution 'that a college for general education be founded in the metropolis, in which, while the various branches of literature and science are made the subjects of instruction, it shall be an essential part of the system to imbue the minds of youth with a knowledge of the doctrines and duties of Christianity as inculcated by the United Church of England and Ireland'.

Subscriptions for the new college were invited and a site adjacent to Somerset House in the Strand was purchased. George IV had promised his patronage and the institution received the name of King's College. It was granted a royal charter of incorporation in 1829 and opened in 1831. The historian of the College tells us that the curriculum consisted initially of 'religion and morals, classical literature, mathematics, natural history, logic, English literature and composition, the principles of commerce and general history. To these will be added instruction in modern foreign languages, and in subjects connected with particular professions, as medicine and surgery, jurisprudence, etc.'.

12   The original London University, which became University College in 1836. This print of 1828 is inscribed 'to Henry Brougham, Esq., MP, and Thomas Campbell, Esq., to whose united exertions London is indebted for her University'.

The new institution had a rather slow start. In the first session there were 114 students and by 1836–1837, the numbers had risen to only 183.

Thus two rival colleges came to be built in London: King's College and the older college known then as London University. Each was based on different principles. The older college enjoyed the support of the Whigs and non-conformists while King's received the backing of the Tories and the Church of England. Neither had been given power to grant degrees and many people felt that the situation was unsatisfactory. Efforts were made to unite the colleges but each proposal in this direction was rejected by King's. Eventually the agitation of both colleges for power to grant degrees, together with the likelihood that still further colleges would be established, obliged the Government to arrange a compromise.

On 28 November 1836 in a move to avoid the multiplication of small universities, a third institution was set up by royal charter. The University of London was created with power 'to perform all the functions of the Examiners in the Senate House of Cambridge'. In other words, it was given the power to grant degrees in arts, law and medicine.

On the same day as the grant of the charter, the college in Gower Street (the so-called 'University of London') was renamed University College. The new University was established in the form of a Chancellor and a Senate of 36 fellows appointed for life by the Crown. Although it was empowered to hold *examinations* and grant degrees in arts, law and medicine, it was not given *teaching* functions. The two colleges – University and King's – were confined to teaching and to private examinations. The power to examine and grant degrees on the results of the collegiate teaching lay with the University of London.

Development

The charter of 1836 made provision for colleges other than King's or University College to be allowed subsequently to submit candidates for the University examinations. In 1850 this provision was implemented when a large number of institutions were affiliated to the University. The number of arts colleges increased from the original two to nearly fifty and the number of medical schools approached one hundred. Many of the latter were located throughout the country so that affiliation ceased to have any real significance. Candidates for University examinations had to spend two years of certified study in one of the affiliated colleges.

The compromise achieved by the creation of London University in 1836 did not end the battle over Church influence, and Thomas Arnold resigned from the University Senate in 1839 in protest against its refusal to make examination in scripture compulsory for undergraduates. Nevertheless, it remains true that the new University was instrumental in breaking the Anglican grip on university studies.

In 1858 a new charter introduced a revolutionary change in the examining system. The practice of admitting candidates for degrees who had attended a course of study at an affiliated college was abandoned. In its place, the University adopted 'the comprehensive principle of testing acquired knowledge by strict examination, with reasonable evidence of antecedent continuous study'. Henceforth a candidate for a degree (except for a medical degree) could take his whole course of study how and where he chose. There were no conditions as to residence or attendance at any colleges. Degrees were conferred on anyone who could pass the examinations at the required standard and who could pay the examination fee.

The charter of 1858 contained two further innovations. The first was the creation of 'convocation' (that is, a body consisting of graduates of the university recruited from doctors, masters and bachelors on payment of a nominal fee) to share in the administration of the university. The other was the creation of the science faculty. In 1859 London became the first university in England to introduce degrees in science.

It is of interest to note here that London was the first university to open its degrees to women candidates. The capital city had been the centre of the feminist education movement led by Frances Mary Buss, Dorothea Beale and Mrs Emily Davies. In 1867 the university admitted women to a series of special examinations but in 1878 it threw open to them all degrees, exhibitions and scholarships upon the same conditions as men.

A university which existed only to examine and confer degrees drew a great deal of criticism. People like Matthew Arnold believed the teaching in a university to be

13 The Hunterian Museum was part of the Royal College of Surgeons and intended for the use of doctors and medical students.

more important than the function of examining. He described the university as 'a mere *collegium* or Board of Examiners'. Other criticisms centred round the fact that the university did not concern itself with the training of students. The teaching staffs of the colleges which submitted students for London degrees complained they had no voice in drawing up syllabuses or setting examination papers.

The University Senate refused to yield to pressure to allow college representatives join its board. Consequently the two original colleges decided to seek charters of their own. The Royal Colleges of Physicians and Surgeons also combined to press for the right to grant medical degrees.

It was, perhaps, inevitable that with nothing to unite them, the university and the London colleges should drift apart. The university developed its examining system while University College and King's struggled to reach high academic standards unaided by the prestige of full university rank. Eventually the matters of dispute reached such proportions that the Government appointed a Royal Commission to examine the various issues under the chairmanship of Lord Selborne. The Commission's report was published in May 1889. The Commissioners recommended that the power to confer degrees was *not* to be given to colleges but should remain the prerogative of the university. The report also recommended that the university should become a *teaching* as well as an *examining* institution, but the details of how this was to be achieved were left undecided.

Consequently the University Senate entered into negotiations with the colleges but the scheme it evolved for turning itself into a teaching university was opposed by both University and King's Colleges. It was not altogether surprising that the University failed to devise a scheme. The problem of producing order out of chaos at that time has been described by R. L. Archer as 'the most complex that has ever presented itself in academic history'. There were more students in London than in any other city in the British Empire, yet they were scattered amongst a host of institutions which were often utterly dissimilar to each other. These institutions existed without any organic connection, with totally different histories, and many of them were probably unaware of each other's existence. As Professor Archer wrote, 'public opinion came to look on London University as a steamroller that had broken down and stuck in the mud, if we take a metaphor suited to its unwieldy bulk, or as Humpty-Dumpty after his fall, if we think rather of its fragmentary condition'. In addition to these problems, reform was opposed by supporters of the existing system who feared the results of placing the University under the control of an academic body dominated by local college interests.

This unhappy state of affairs caused University and King's College to consider a plan to leave the existing University and found a new teaching university which should be named Gresham University. The Government intervened once again and appointed a second Royal Commission in 1892 – the Gresham Commission with Earl Cowper as chairman – which reported in 1894.

The Commissioners favoured a single university for London and generally, supported the conclusions of the Selborne Commission. The failure earlier of

14 Sidney and Beatrice Webb, the left-wing intellectuals who founded the London School of Economics and wrote books on political and economic issues.

negotiations between the University and the colleges caused the Commissioners to recommend legislation as the only means of implementing the changes. Thus in 1898 the Government passed the University of London Act.

Under this Act the University was reconstituted as a *teaching* body. Provision was made for 'internal' students who attended courses in colleges which became 'schools' of the teaching university. They included 24 institutions of various types. In addition to University College and King's College, there were the London teaching hospitals, a number of theological colleges, the London School of Economics (founded in 1895) and women's colleges such as Bedford and the Royal Holloway College. University College and King's were given representation on the University Senate. They and the other schools carried on the bulk of the teaching and remained legally and financially independent of the Senate. However, with a view to strengthening the reconstituted university, University College in 1905 and King's College in 1908, surrendered their legal independence and in

23

1907 and 1910 respectively, became incorporated in the University. This example was not followed by other schools.

A feature of the new constitution was the recognition of individual teachers, under whom students could follow courses of instruction leading to internal degrees, in a number of institutions in London not otherwise connected with the University.

Under the Act the former examination system of the University was placed under an external council. Examinations for 'external' students continued and as before the University did not concern itself with their training. They were allowed to work privately or in some institution along the lines of a prescribed syllabus and sit for the examinations. Thus there was created a dual system of internal and external degrees.

The administration of the heterogeneous institutions which formed the reconstituted university posed problems, not the least of which was that of finding

15   The administrative centre for the University has been housed on a number of sites. In 1868 the Government provided premises in Burlington Gardens (shown here); in 1900 a move was made to the Imperial Institute (now Imperial College) at South Kensington; and in 1936 the administration was moved to its present site in Bloomsbury.

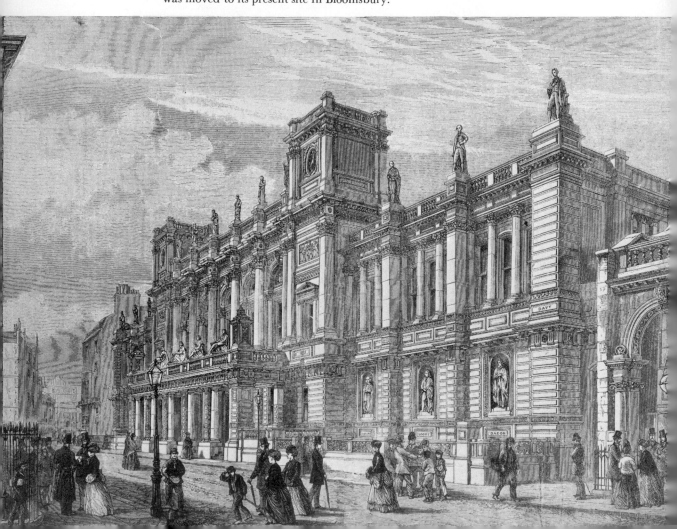

16 The Senate House, London University, is the building with the white tower in the centre, and forms the nucleus for the widely scattered colleges. Looking along the diagonal, top right to bottom left, to the right of the Senate House is the British Museum, and to the left is Birkbeck College, then the University of London Union. Further building has taken place around the site since this photograph of 1955.

suitable administrative headquarters. For the first thirty years of its life, the University had had no fixed location until in 1868 the Government built premises for it in Burlington Gardens. In 1900, following the reorganisation, it was housed in part of the buildings belonging to the Imperial Institute at South Kensington.

Other administrative problems were resolved in successive stages dating from the appointment of the Haldane Commission in 1909 to the passing of an Act in 1926.

The Haldane Commission was appointed to review the whole position of the reconstituted university, but its recommendations were suspended by the outbreak of the first World War in 1914. In 1924 a Government committee reconsidered the Commission's report and recommended the following changes:

(1) the creation of a new body, the University Court, to control finance,

(2) closer association of the schools with the University, mainly through representation on the Senate, which was to remain the supreme governing body of the University in all academic matters.

These changes formed the basis of a new constitution which was created by the University of London Act passed in 1926.

The increase in size of the University had made inadequate the accommodation at the Imperial Institute. The need for permanent head-quarters on a central site had been noted by the Haldane Commission and the provision of new headquarters became a major issue of policy. In particular there was a need for a central library.

In 1927 a considerable area of land in Bloomsbury was acquired by the University and a group of buildings housing the administrative offices was erected immediately north of the British Museum and not far from University College in Gower Street. The group is dominated by a great tower which contains the University Library. These buildings, the first of which was completed in 1936 exactly one hundred years after the sealing of William IV's charter to the University, stand as a symbol of unity to the widely scattered University. Their cost was met to a large extent by grants from the Government and local authorities, from City companies, banks, business firms, private donors and the Rockefeller Foundation of America. Further expansion on this site and the extension of the site itself has permitted the establishment of a 'university precinct' in or near which a substantial proportion of the University's activities find a focus.

The new constitution in 1926 retained the dual system of internal and external degrees and some controversy still surrounds the latter. Critics claim that the courses of study are drawn up by persons having no links with the institutions in which these studies are pursued. The external system, it is said, is an unsatisfactory substitute for examinations set by teachers acquainted with the way in which candidates have been taught. Other critics have pounced on the fact that private students entering for the examinations miss the benefits of a university training, namely, daily contact with other students and with distinguished teachers.

On the other hand, supporters of the external degree system assert that its benefits outweigh the disadvantages. It has provided the possibility of academic qualification for many thousands of people who had no opportunity of entering a university. In addition it has provided a means whereby advanced work can be examined in institutions striving for full university status. The development of new universities in this country (such as Nottingham, Exeter, Southampton, Leicester and Hull) and throughout the Commonwealth would have been hindered if initially, they had been unable to enter their students for degree examinations at London.

Despite these arguments for and against the system, it is beyond dispute that the system whereby any person of any nationality may register as an external student, and present himself for an examination of a standard exactly parallel with that taken by internal students, is one of the notable educational inventions of the nineteenth century. 'Whatever may be its future', declared the Robbins Committee on Higher Education, 'its honourable place in academic history is a matter of common consent.'

During the twentieth century a great expansion of the teaching university has taken place. In 1900 there were 18 schools of the university and in 1902–1903 it had 2,000 internal students. In 1952–1953 it comprised 34 schools (18 non-medical and 16 medical) and 10 university institutes. The latter are centres for specialised postgraduate work but in two of them – the Courtauld Institute of Art and the School of Slavonic and East European Studies – courses are provided for under-graduates. There were 22,000 internal students of whom 4,000 were in 'institutions having recognised teachers' not organically connected with the University. In 1971–1972 the University comprised 50 schools and 14 institutes and there were over 37,000 internal students.

The external work of the University continued to expand after 1900. While many technical college and private students continued to register, the University was increasingly concerned with fostering the growth of university colleges at home and abroad. They were provided with advisory services and an examination and degree system during their period of growth towards full and independent university status. In 1971–1972 the number of students registered for external degree and diploma examinations was 33,000.

Summary

Whereas nineteenth century Oxford and Cambridge were national universities connected with upper class careers in politics, administration and the liberal professions, offering a general education designed to mould character and prepare their students for a gentlemanly style of life, London addressed itself to the needs of the professional and industrial middle classes, taking most of its students from its own area and offering them a more vocational training for middle class careers. Degree courses were directed especially towards the newer technological and professional occupations such as chemistry, electrical engineering and the scientific civil service.

Today London is unique among universities in a number of ways. It is the largest university in the United Kingdom with approximately 37,000 full-time internal students. It is the only university which confers external degrees, a system providing the part-time student or the student who cannot, for various reasons, become a member of the University with an opportunity of gaining qualifications of a high academic standard.

The University has three distinct types of institutions which are constituent parts of the whole. There are the *University Institutes* dealing with specialised and mainly postgraduate work; the *Schools of the University* which provide the bulk of the teaching; and various institutions such as the Royal College of Music where the University has 'recognised teachers'. These institutions have no other link with the University.

Unlike the colleges of Oxford and Cambridge, the colleges in London are geographically dispersed. Two of them – Royal Holloway College near Staines and Wye College near Canterbury are outside London altogether. As a result of the special circumstances which moulded its growth, the University of London stands in many respects in a class by itself.

FURTHER READING
G. S. Wilson, *The University of London and its Colleges* U.T.P.
T. L. Humberstone, *University Reform in London* Allen & Unwin
F. J. C. Hearnshaw, *The Centenary History of King's College* Harrap
H. H. Bellot, *University College, London 1826–1926*
Annual Calendar of the University of London

3 The Civic Universities

The word 'civic' describes the group of universities founded to bring the benefits of higher education to provincial life. They can be conveniently divided into two groups—the older and the younger civic universities.

The older civic universities of England (Durham, Manchester, Birmingham, Liverpool, Leeds, Sheffield and Bristol) were founded in the nineteenth century or before the outbreak of the first World War in 1914. They were originally intended to serve local needs but have developed into national institutions drawing students from all over the country. Steady expansion has meant that they now accommodate over a third of all the university students in England.

17 A strong stimulus to the establishment of provincial colleges was provided by the work of the Mechanics' Institutes. These institutions had their origins in Glasgow in the eighteenth century. George Birkbeck founded the London Mechanics' Institute in 1805 and the movement spread rapidly throughout the country. The Institutes were an important step in the development of scientific and technical instruction and they helped to draw attention to the educational needs of provincial areas.

The second group comprises the younger civic universities. Reading, Nottingham, Southampton, Hull, Exeter and Leicester were founded as university colleges in the years before and after the first World War. Until they received university status (Reading in 1926, the others after the end of the second World War in 1945), they taught for the London external degree. Since they became universities they have grown rapidly. One university college was founded immediately after the second World War. This was Keele which became a University in 1962.

None of the civic universities was founded as such; they have gradually evolved out of colleges of various types. Charters were not granted until the Privy Council was satisfied that their financial position was stable enough to allow them to carry on university work in a proper manner. They have owed their origin and growth largely to the generosity of private individuals and have been supported by business firms and local authorities. Treasury grants have also supplemented local resources.

The Older Civic Universities

DURHAM

Plans for a university in the north of England date from the sixteenth century and a broadsheet dated 1596 recording details of a proposed university is in the library of Ripon Cathedral. The broadsheet gives details about the teachers and their duties. For example, it was suggested that lectures might be given to the crowds who gathered on market days. In spite of strong support received from the Queen and prominent nobles and clergy, the scheme petered out.

In 1641 Lord Fairfax petitioned Parliament for a university at Manchester. The petition began:

> That whereas the want of an university in the northern parts of this kingdom, both in this and former ages, hath been apprehended a great prejudice to the kingdom in general, but a greater misery and unhappiness to these countries in particular, many ripe and hopeful wits being utterly lost for want of education, some being unable, others unwilling, to commit their children of tender and unsettled age so far from their own eyes, to the sole care and tuition of strangers; we therefore humbly crave leave to offer unto your pious care and wise consideration the necessity of a third university, and the convenience of such a foundation in the town of Manchester, for the future advancement of piety and good learning amongst us.

Supporters of the petition pressed their case by pointing out the long distances from the North to Oxford and Cambridge; the high cost of student life at these universities; and the existence of a number of people who would make generous gifts to endow a third university.

Unfortunately the petition was drawn up at the time when King and Parliament were in conflict. Furthermore the City of York sent its own petition to Parliament. The result of the rivalry was that neither petition was granted. Later an additional factor defeating both claims was Oliver Cromwell's preference for Durham as the centre for a new university. Accordingly a college was set up in Durham in 1656. It was to be known as the Provost, Fellows and Scholars of the College of Durham, and its income was to come from the cathedral endowments. Two years later the College petitioned Richard Cromwell for a charter to proclaim it a university. This step was opposed by Oxford and Cambridge but before the dispute could be resolved, the College of Durham was dissolved. At the Restoration of 1660, the Church was restored to its old privileges and endowments; the Cromwellian college was swept away.

Nearly two centuries were to elapse before the University of Durham was successfully founded. It was established by Act of Parliament in 1832 which enabled 'the Dean and Chapter of Durham to appropriate part of their church to the establishment of a university in connection therewith'.

Before the coming of the railways the country areas of the northern counties of Westmorland, Cumberland, and Durham were rather isolated from the rest of the country. The population was spread thinly throughout these areas and the clergy were, generally, both poor and inadequately educated. The foundation of the University was an attempt to remedy this state of affairs, in that it was concerned mainly with the training of the Anglican clergy. The University was residential and began in the Norman castle which fronts the cathedral. Its curriculum was modelled on that of Oxford and Cambridge but the fees charged to students were much lower. A charter was granted in 1837 empowering the new University to award degrees.

In 1832 a College of Medicine was founded at Newcastle-upon-Tyne and became affiliated to Durham University in 1852. Armstrong College – a college of science situated in Newcastle – also became associated with the University in 1874. At the end of the nineteenth century, therefore, the University comprised three separate, self-governing institutions. In 1908 an Act of Parliament reorganised the University into the Durham division and the Newcastle division. Control by the Cathedral authorities, which had remained since 1832 was ended.

With the passing of an Act in 1963, Durham University, for the first time since 1852, became confined to Durham. The original bias towards arts and theology has been swallowed up by an increasing emphasis on science. By the same Act the University of Newcastle-upon-Tyne acquired a separate existence on 1 August 1963.

MANCHESTER

Owens College opened at Manchester in 1851 as the result of a bequest by a local merchant named John Owens. The aim of the college was to provide instruction 'in such branches of learning and science as are now and may be hereafter, usually

18 The nineteenth century civic universities were the product of local initiative. Finance was provided by funds raised locally in the form of either private donations or public subscription. Owens College opened at Manchester in 1851 as the result of a bequest of £97,000 by the local merchant (shown here) named John Owens.

taught in the English universities'. Students were prepared for London external degrees and there were no religious tests for admission. The college had an uncertain start. During the session 1857–1858 its numbers fell to 93, including evening students, and in a leading article the *Manchester Guardian* referred to it as 'a mortifying failure'.

The chief reason for the low numbers was the lack of a sound system of secondary education. Hence students were ill-prepared to proceed to higher education. Faced with this depressing situation the college authorities were under some pressure to lower academic standards, but they decided against this course. Their decision was justified when the high standards set by Owens College resulted in an improvement in the quality of secondary teaching in Manchester. By 1864 there were 127 day and 312 evening students and the improvement in numbers encouraged the college authorities to raise funds for rebuilding. The response was generous and a Bill was presented to Parliament to obtain authorisation for extension and the grant of a new constitution. In 1871 Owens College received its new constitution and the power to admit women as students. The new buildings of the College were opened in 1874 and the number of students increased to over 1,000.

Inevitably the growth of the College caused its authorities to plan for changing it into a local university with the power of conferring its own degrees.

However, events were happening in Yorkshire which were to affect the development of Owens College. In 1874 a college of science and technology was founded at Leeds. It was called the Yorkshire College of Science and its establishment was the result of a number of factors, such as the growing appreciation of the value of scientific and technical education; the influences of the Leeds Mechanics' Institute; and the revival of secondary education in the area.

The aim of the college was 'to supply instruction in those sciences which are applicable to the Manufactures, Engineering, Mining and Agriculture of the County of York; also in such Arts and Languages as are cognate to the foregoing purpose'. At the inauguration ceremony in 1875, Mr W. E. Forster, MP, prophesied that the college would be the start of a provincial university. An article in the *Bradford Observer* also looked forward to the time when 'the College of Science has grown into a great Yorkshire University'. Well over 300 students attended the first year's course of lectures and the Cambridge University Extension Committee (which had been set up in Leeds) helped to consolidate the new institution by handing over its functions to the new College in 1877.

This was the position at Leeds when Owens College, Manchester petitioned the Privy Council for the grant of a university charter. The request met with considerable opposition from Yorkshire and the Yorkshire College sent its own petition to the Privy Council. The Council was asked not to grant a charter to Owens College but instead to create a new university into which Owens College and other institutions might be incorporated. It was also urged that if the new university was given the name of a town or person, the effect would be to localise it.

After negotiations between the two Colleges, it was agreed that if Manchester gave up the hope of a local name for the new university, Owens College should be named as the first college constituting the university. In 1880 the Victoria University received its charter and Owens College was incorporated in it. The new University granted its own degrees and was independent of London.

University College, Liverpool was founded in 1881. As a result of a town meeting convened in 1879 the Liverpool Corporation granted a site and £50,000 was raised by subscription. In January 1882 University College opened in a disused lunatic asylum in the midst of a slum district. Two years later it was united with Owens College in the federal Victoria University. In 1887 the Yorkshire College became a member of the confederation.

Federal universities tend to be unwieldy and their organisation is difficult. In 1890 Leeds and Liverpool quarrelled violently over the proposal that a chair of theology should be established. Other matters of friction included the continual travelling from Leeds and Liverpool to Manchester for meetings of examiners and of the Court of Governors. Consequently the Victoria University broke up in 1903 and Manchester and Liverpool received charters of their own. Leeds was left as

19 The inaugural meeting of the new university college at Liverpool in January 1882. The speaker is the Principal, Professor Rendall.

the sole member of the Victoria University and sought to obtain the title of Yorkshire University. The proposal was opposed by University College, Sheffield and the Privy Council preferred the title of the University of Leeds. The latter came into existence in April 1904.

BIRMINGHAM

Birmingham University evolved from a college founded by Josiah Mason in 1880. Mason was a manufacturer of split rings and pens and his aim was to 'provide enlarged means of scientific instruction on the scale required by the necessities of the town and district . . . upon terms which render it easily available by persons of all classes'. At this time Birmingham was the centre of the hardware trade which had been steadily losing ground to American products.

Mason acquired a site in Edmund Street and the college was formally opened in 1880 after the expenditure by Mason of nearly £200,000. Like Owens at Manchester, Mason repudiated all religious tests. Mason Science College was intended to offer a purely scientific and utilitarian training. In fact, literary education and theology were rigidly excluded in its Foundation deed. However as the students were preparing for London degrees which required literary subjects, Mason was obliged to modify his position. Hence the word 'Science' disappeared from the title of the college.

33

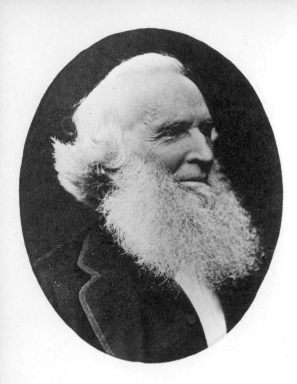

20 Sir Josiah Mason.

21 In 1880 Mason founded a Science College which developed into Birmingham University.

Joseph Chamberlain, the dynamic Birmingham MP, became president of the Mason College in 1898 and he determined to change it into a civic university. He appealed for an endowment of £500,000 so that application could be made for a charter. By February 1899 the target figure had been exceeded by £76,500 and application was made for a charter, which was sealed on 24 March 1900. Birmingham was the first provincial university to carry the title of a particular city.

SHEFFIELD

At Sheffield a local steelmaster named Mark Firth endowed a college in 1879 to house the University Extension Movement. His generosity was so liberal that it retained his name till it merged in 1897 with the local medical school and a technical college to form University College, Sheffield. The endowments were increased and its governing body thought of applying for admission to the Victoria University. The latter was, however, at that time in a state of disruption and after raising sufficient funds to erect new buildings, Sheffield received its charter and became an independent university in 1905.

22 Sheffield University developed from a college founded in 1879 by Mark Firth, a local steelmaster.

BRISTOL

The last civic foundation of the nineteenth century was at Bristol. In 1876 a College of Science for the West of England was established by W. L. Carpenter, W. Proctor Baker and Lewis Fry. In their circular convening a public meeting to discuss the proposed new college, they wrote:

'It is generally admitted that the prosperity of British industry must in future greatly depend upon the proper scientific and technical training of those by whom the commerce and manufactures of the country will be carried out. . . . At the same time there is a growing conviction that culture in all the subjects which form the staple of university teaching should be made more widely accessible.'

Civic support and private donations flowed in and in August 1876 University College came into being. The University of Bristol was chartered in May 1909.

STATE ASSISTANCE

The menace of German and American competition, based as it was upon superior institutions for industrial education, continued to be publicised. T. H. Huxley wrote to the *Times* on 21 March 1887 'We are entering, indeed we have already entered, upon the most serious struggle for existence to which this country was ever committed. The latter years of the century promise to see us in an industrial war of far more serious import than the military wars of its opening years . . . .'

To promote victory in this industrial race, the National Association for the Promotion of Technical Education was formed and a vigorous campaign for state aid to provincial colleges was set in motion. 'They have proved their value' wrote Benjamin Jowett, 'and, like every other educational institution they have proved that they cannot live without external help. The only help that is likely to be permanent and that will enable them to feel secure is help from the State.' In response to these pressures, the Government passed the Technical Instruction Act 1889 giving local authorities power to levy a rate specifically for technical education.

Another important step to foster civic university colleges was taken when in 1889 the sum of £15,000 was entered in the Treasury Estimates for distribution to university colleges. With the exception of Oxford, Cambridge and Manchester, all these foundations were in financial straits at this period, funds from private sources having been practically exhausted. A committee was appointed to advise on the distribution of the grant, and this meant, in fact, the appointment of a University Grants Committee.

A year later, in 1890 a further windfall from the State fell into the coffers of the civic colleges. The secretary of the Technical Education Association persuaded the Chancellor of the Exchequer to divert £750,000 to the further assistance of technical education. This sum had been originally intended to provide compensation for publicans deprived of their licences as a result of legislation reducing the number of public houses. Some of this 'whisky money' went to the university colleges and provided much needed finance.

The Younger Civic Universities

Unlike the large cities of the North of England, *Reading* had no densely peopled area surrounding it from which to draw its students. It has been, therefore, less provincial in character than the other modern universities. Undergraduates were recruited from all parts of the country and Reading developed a system of halls of residence from the start – a new thing in the civic universities. Another characteristic of Reading is its close attention to agricultural studies. University College was opened in 1892 and it originated from Oxford University Extension work. A charter was granted to the University of Reading in 1926.

Like Reading, *Nottingham* owed its origin to the University Extension classes carried out in that city. Nottingham was the first town to run an Extension course and it was organised in a re-built Mechanics' Institute. Out of this movement and with the support of trade unionists, private donors and the civic authorities (who

23 A University College was founded in Nottingham in 1881. Mr Gladstone addressed the meeting at the laying of the memorial stone.

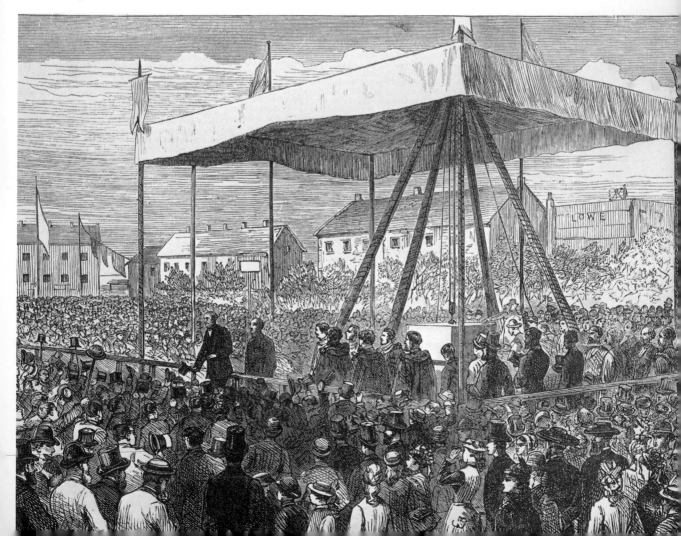

24 *(above)* University College, Nottingham moved to a new block of buildings in 1928, the result of a benefaction by Sir Jesse Boot (afterwards Lord Trent).

25 *(below)* The founding of the University College of North Staffordshire in 1949 marked a break with traditional policy in that it was given the power to grant its own degree. In 1962 the college became Keele University. The photograph shows a tutor in English with a group of students.

levied a rate on the town for the purpose), a University College was founded in 1881. As the result of a generous benefaction by Sir Jesse Boot (afterwards Lord Trent) the College moved to a new block of buildings in 1928. University status was granted in 1948.

Southampton received university status in 1954, *Hull* in 1954, and *Exeter* and *Leicester* in 1957.

The University College of North Staffordshire which received a charter in 1949 and opened in 1950 was a break with traditional policy. Up to this date, university colleges prepared their students for the external degrees of the University of London. The new university college was given the power to grant the degree of B.A., under the sponsorship of three other universities, until it became *Keele University* in 1962.

Summary

The universities which have grown out of the provincial colleges were mainly situated in industrial areas, and for that reason have tended to develop a scientific or technological bias. New faculties and departments have been evolved such as economics, engineering, textile and leather working, dyeing and brewing, agriculture and horticulture. At the same time all the universities provide a full range of arts and pure science subjects.

The one major weakness of the provincial university system is the difficulty of developing a community life comparable to that evolved by the ancient residential universities. Students who live at home or in lodgings are 'day students' and miss the educational experience of living in a college. The provision of halls of residence is an attempt to counter this weakness and Reading in particular, has observed the principle of residence from the first.

FURTHER READING

W. H. G. Armytage, *Civic Universities* Ernest Benn

A. D. Chapman, *A History of the University of Sheffield* Oxford University Press

H. B. Charlton, *Portrait of a University 1851–1951* Manchester University Press

W. B. Gillie, *A New University: A. D. Lindsay and the Keele Experiment* Chatto & Windus

A. H. Shimmin, *The University of Leeds* Cambridge University Press

4 Scotland and Wales

Scotland

There were no universities in Scotland before the fifteenth century. In the early Middle Ages, Scottish students seeking higher education travelled to England and the Continent. At Padua there was a group of Scottish students and a Scots college at the University of Paris was started in 1326 by the Bishop of Moray. In 1266 Balliol College, Oxford was founded for the purpose of maintaining poor Scottish students.

Journeys overseas were dangerous because of the risk of attack by pirates; travel to England was equally as hazardous due to the almost continual warfare between England and Scotland. Inevitably these difficulties gave rise to plans for the establishment of a university in Scotland. Events abroad brought the matter to fulfilment in the early fifteenth century. In 1408 the University of Paris quarrelled with

26 Balliol College, Oxford was founded in 1266 for the purpose of maintaining poor Scottish students.

the Pope and as Scotland remained loyal to the papacy, Scottish students were expelled from Paris. They returned home and congregated at St Andrews, seat of the greatest bishopric and the largest monastery in Scotland. Lectures for them were organised by the prior of the monastery and the archdeacon of the cathedral. So successful were these lectures that the Bishop, Henry Wardlaw, formally incorporated the scholars as a 'universitas' on 25 January 1412. In the following year Bishop Wardlaw obtained a charter from the Pope for the foundation of a *studium generale*. The latter was modelled upon the University of Paris and its members were divided into four Nations based upon the district from which they came, namely, Fife, Lothian, Angus and Alban. The new University received support from King James I who confirmed its establishment by issuing a royal charter and exempted its members from the payment of taxes.

In its early days, the University of St Andrews had few students or teachers. Teaching took place in hired buildings and students lodged in the town. However, private benefactors endowed a number of buildings, and by the time of the

27 King's College, Aberdeen.

Reformation the University comprised three colleges: St Salvator's, St Leonard's and St Mary's. All were founded by bishops.

Two other universities, those of Glasgow and Aberdeen, were founded in the fifteenth century.

In 1450 William Turnbull, Bishop of Glasgow, persuaded King James II to petition the Pope for a charter authorising the establishment of a new university. The petition was successful. The development of Glasgow University followed a similar pattern to that of St Andrew's. There were no buildings, initially, for teaching purposes, and students were taught in the cathedral and other churches. Later, Lord Hamilton gave four acres of land to the University, but with true Scottish caution, he wrote into the charter the right of his heirs to take back the property into their possession. The option was not exercised and a college endowed by the family was used for the ensuing 400 years.

The University of Aberdeen was founded in 1494. King James IV petitioned the Pope for his authority to establish a new university and supported the petition with a powerful argument. At that time the people of the Highlands were ignorant and untutored, mainly because of the remoteness of the area where they lived. Consequently there was a shortage of good candidates for the ministry of the Church. The establishment of a university would, it was felt, help to meet this need. The petition was successful. The new University benefited from the experience acquired by its Bishop when he had served as Rector of Glasgow University. Bishop Elphinstone had seen the difficulties resulting from lack of funds to establish permanent teaching facilities and he took good care that Aberdeen had sufficient endowments in this respect. Hence in its early days, the University of Aberdeen had a more flourishing career than the earlier Scottish universities.

The foundation of three universities in the fifteenth century was a remarkable achievement for a country with such a scanty population. The entire population was probably barely half a million people and towns, generally, were small. In 1450, for example, Glasgow had only about 1,500 inhabitants. Most of the people were poor and their land was disturbed by war with England and by rebellion of the nobility against the king.

Not surprisingly, the universities were themselves poor and the students, many of whom started their courses about the age of 13, lived on very little, often in squalid lodgings. Life in the colleges was strict. The working day began before 6 a.m. and attendance was required at many religious services.

It is probable at this early period that the teaching in the universities was little in advance of that given in the grammar schools. Nevertheless the establishment of the early universities was important in that they provided the basis from which future development could spring.

The University of Edinburgh dates from 1582. Its foundation reflected the efforts of the Town Council to introduce an institution for higher education. The Town Council retained control of the University until the latter was granted its independence by the Universities (Scotland) Act of 1858.

The Scottish Universities in the sixteenth and seventeenth centuries differed considerably from the Universities of England.

In the first place, the Scottish Universities were to a greater extent, universities of the people. A less rigid distinction between elementary and secondary schools meant that pupils progressed to university studies from the parochial schools as well as the grammar schools. Hence Scottish students comprised all classes of the population – sons of nobles, lairds, ministers, farmers and mechanics. The universities never became, as the two oldest English universities did, the preserve of one social moneyed class.

Scottish students entered university at an earlier age than English students. Many entered at eleven or twelve and graduated at sixteen. The majority were ignorant of Greek or Latin and elementary classes in these subjects had to be started during the eighteenth century. Poverty was such that in the seventeenth century large numbers of students moved out of the colleges (where they could not afford even the moderate charges) to live in mean garrets. 'There are only forty scholars that lodge in the College,' wrote an English traveller to Glasgow in 1704 'but there are two or three hundred that belong to it'. Even as late as the nineteenth century, doles of a few pence were given to the young students as they travelled to college. Many existed throughout the university session on a supply of oat and barley meal.

Like their students, the teachers were also poor. Salaries paid to professors were small. In the early eighteenth century, the Professor of Mathematics at Aberdeen was paid only £10 per annum. His income came from a tax levied on the sales of ale in the town, so that it could rightly be said that the teaching of mathematics in the University depended on the quantity of beer drunk by the citizens. Salaries improved during the century and a professor's income was augmented by fees paid by his students. Thus in 1764, Professor Reid at Glasgow was able to write 'I have touched £70 in fees and may possibly make out the hundred this session'. If the cost of living had not been low, professors would have been unable to live on the their incomes.

The improvement in salaries during the eighteenth century was matched by an improvement in the intellectual life of the universities. Scholars such as David Hume, Thomas Reid and Adam Smith were renowned for their learning far beyond their own lecture rooms. At this period theology, law, science and most of all, medicine, came into their own. The progress of the latter was outstanding.

In both Edinburgh and Glasgow the practise of medicine was associated with the barbers. In Edinburgh there existed the Incorporation of Surgeons and Barbers while in Glasgow the Faculty of Physicians and Surgeons included barbers. At this time the barbers not only cut hair but also veins and arteries in the common treatment of 'bleeding' a person. In consequence they had to have some understanding of human anatomy. The red and blue stripes on the modern barber's pole serve as a reminder of the close association that existed between surgeons and barbers; the red stripes represent the arteries and the blue stripes suggest the

28 During the eighteenth century Scottish scholars were renowned for their learning far beyond their own lecture rooms. For example, Adam Smith was Professor of Logic and Moral Philosophy at Glasgow and his *Wealth of Nations*, published in 1776, is considered to be a landmark in the development of economics as a subject of study.

veins. However, during the seventeenth century, the surgeons and barbers tended to break away from each other and in 1727 the two professions separated. The principal reason for the rift was the increasingly contemptuous attitude of the surgeons towards their more humble brethren.

After the separation in 1727 the medical schools of Glasgow and Edinburgh developed rapidly. In 1824 a dispute arose in the University of Edinburgh over the introduction of midwifery. The University Senate objected to its introduction, but the Town Council who controlled the University were in favour of the innovation. The controversy caused the Senate to petition for a royal commission, which was appointed in 1826 and took for its enquiry the whole field of Scottish university education. The recommendations of the Commission formed the basis of the University Act 1858.

The main feature of this Act was to change the government of the universities. Previously, the Senate had been the governing body and this comprised the professors. The latter were, therefore, both the teachers and the governors of their institution. Under the Act two new bodies were introduced, namely, the University Court and the General Council. The purposes of the Court were to appoint professors, to regulate fees and to be responsible generally for the internal organisation of the university. The Council was a larger body which was to meet twice a year to discuss measures approved by the Senate or the Court. Despite these changes, the Senate still retained considerable power.

The chief effect of broadening the basis of university government was to bring the curricula more into line with the demands of the modern world. In turn this change led to a considerable increase in students.

44   Two further events towards the close of the nineteenth century are of interest.

29 & 30 Dundee is the newest Scottish University. It was founded in 1881 and affiliated to St Andrews until 1967 when it gained independence. The illustrations show engineering and dental students at work.

The first was the establishment of chairs in the History, Theory and Practice of Education, at Edinburgh and St Andrew's in 1876. These were the first chairs in education to be established in Great Britain. The second event was the admission of women to degrees by the four universities in 1892.

In the twentieth century, the Scottish universities, like those in England, have expanded considerably. Not only has the number of students at the four ancient Scottish Universities increased greatly but three more universities have been created.

The University of Strathclyde became, in 1963, the fifth Scottish university, having developed from the Royal Technical College, Glasgow. The latter had been founded in 1796 in response to pressures for the introduction of technical education.

In July 1964, Stirling was accepted as a new University and admitted its first students in 1967. The Heriot-Watt College in Edinburgh, which was similar to the Royal Technical College at Glasgow, became a University in 1966. University College, Dundee, founded in 1881 was affiliated to the University of St Andrews in 1897. For many years Dundee aimed at becoming a separate university and this ambition was realised in 1967.

31 The first recorded attempt to found a university in Wales was connected with the national rising led by Owen Glendower in the fifteenth century. Glendower petitioned the Pope in 1406 for the establishment of universities for north and south Wales. Their foundation would, he thought, assist him to break from English domination. The plan came to nothing.

Wales

University institutions did not develop in Wales until the nineteenth century. During that period there was a serious decline in the membership of the Church in Wales. Among the measures discussed to remedy the situation was that of founding a Welsh college at which candidates for holy orders could obtain a liberal education fairly cheaply. Dr Burgess, the Bishop of St David's, considered this project would increase the number of clergy and eventually improve the position of the Church. Accordingly, as a result of his efforts St David's College, Lampeter was chartered in 1828. Supporters of the College saw it not only as a training establishment for the clergy but as the foundation on which a Welsh university might eventually be built. Consequently there grew up a demand for St David's to be given authority to award degrees. In 1852 the College was empowered to confer degrees in divinity and, 13 years later, it was given authority to confer the B.A.

Despite the hopes of its founders, St David's College did not develop into the University of Wales. Its close association with the Anglican Church was not acceptable to Welsh Non-conformists who formed a powerful body of opinion in Welsh life.

The initial move for a national university originated, strangely enough, in Yorkshire, where in 1821 a society called 'The Association of Welsh Clergy in the West Riding' was formed. The Association approved the authority given to Lampeter to award degrees, but at the same time, it was felt the establishment of a national university open to all denominations was also desirable. A petition for a Welsh University was presented to Parliament in 1852 and it was followed a year later, by a pamphlet written by B. T. Williams, a Welsh politician. The movement

32 In the seventeenth century there was a movement led by clergymen in the west of England to found a university at Shrewsbury for the purpose of serving Wales. Richard Baxter, the Puritan divine, approached James Berry, Cromwell's Major-General of Hereford, Shropshire and Wales. Berry, wrote Baxter, 'promised me his best assistance, but the want is money'. In spite of Richard Baxter's efforts the project for a western university at Shrewsbury came to nothing.

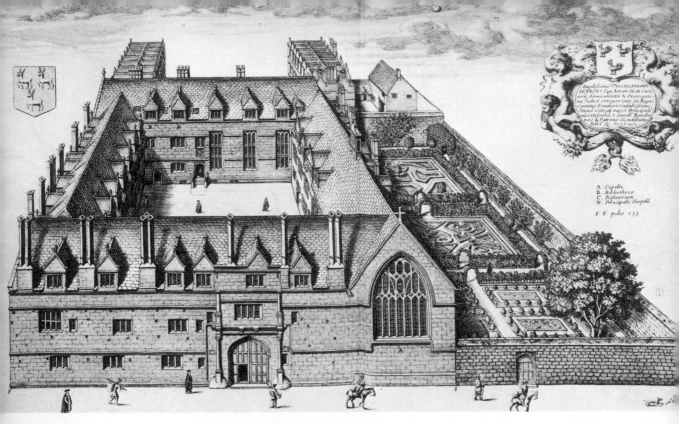

33 The lack of a university in Wales until the nineteenth century meant that Welshmen seeking higher education travelled to Oxford. In 1573 Dr Hugh Price of Brecon founded Jesus College and although neither the founder or the statutes of the college gave preference to the Welsh, Jesus grew to be regarded almost as a Welsh college.

was supported by Sir Hugh Owen, G. O. Morgan, E. J. Salisbury and others. Meetings were held in London and in 1863 a committee was formed to campaign for a national University of Wales.

Four years later the committee managed to acquire the Castle Hotel at Aberystwyth. The building had been planned to serve the increased number of visitors which were expected as a result of the opening of the Cambrian Railway. But in 1867, after £80,000 had already been spent on it, the owner went bankrupt. Seizing the opportunity of a bargain, the committee made an offer of £10,000 for the premises and this was accepted. University College, Aberystwth, opened in 1872. Residential accommodation was provided from the start and students read for external degrees of London University.

The College opened with a deficit of £2,500 but stirred by Sir Hugh Owen, a hundred thousand people rallied with donations totalling £50,000. For ten years the College was supported entirely by the Welsh people, but eventually, financial difficulties caused Welsh Members of Parliament to ask for Government aid. A Departmental Committee under the leadership of Lord Aberdare was appointed to examine the situation and its report recommended a Government grant. Additionally, it was reported that there was need for a proper network of secondary and university education in Wales. Consequently two more colleges, both of

34 The library of St. David's College, Lampeter.

which received Government Grants, were established. Colleges were opened at Cardiff in 1883 and at Bangor in 1884. Government grants were made available to all three Welsh colleges.

The position in 1885, then, was that although Wales possessed three university colleges and the Anglican college at Lampeter, the campaign for a national University of Wales had not yet been successful.

The report of Lord Aberdare's Committee had shown Welsh secondary education to be in a deplorable state. Out of a total population of just over a million and a half, only about four thousand boys received some form of secondary education. The recommendations of the Committee in this respect were eventually embodied in the Welsh Intermediate Education Act of 1889. This Act made use of the new local government machinery of the county and county borough councils established by the Local Government Act, 1888. The local authorities were to appoint education committees to provide secondary and technical education in their areas. Thus there came into existence in Wales a system of secondary or intermediate schools, as they were called – intermediate because their education was between that of the elementary schools and that of the universities. The Act was well received and the results of the reorganisation were to produce a large number of pupils who were qualified to take courses at universities. The number of girls, for example, receiving secondary education increased from 260 in 1880 to 3,400 in 1898. Between 1890 and 1900, 64 intermediate schools were opened. The

49

result of the 1889 Act was to introduce a national system of secondary education some 13 years earlier than in England.

Improved secondary schools brought about renewed demands for a national university. In 1888 a conference of the three university colleges recommended the creation of a federal university similar to the Victoria University. (See Chapter 3). Five years later the federal University of Wales was established (with power to award its own degrees) comprising the three colleges of Aberystwyth, Bangor and Cardiff.

Between the first and second World Wars, the University College of Swansea (1920) and the Welsh National School of Medicine (1931) joined the federation. These colleges were joined by the Cardiff Institute of Science and Technology in 1967 and St David's College, Lampeter in 1969. The University of Wales remains today as a federal University with seven constituent colleges.

FURTHER READING
R. G. Cant, *A Short History of the University of St Andrews* Oliver & Boyd
J. Coutts, *A History of the University of Glasgow* Jas. Macleshouse
T. I. Ellis, *The Development of High Education in Wales* Wrexham
B. E. Evans, *The University of Wales* Cardiff

5 Universities of the Sixties

The 1960s witnessed the greatest single expansion of higher education that this country has ever known. This expansion took a number of forms; existing universities were enlarged; new universities developed from existing institutions; and seven completely new universities were founded.

The Technological Universities

Technology is the scientific study of the industrial arts, and the technological universities developed out of the system of technical education.

Between the two World Wars a number of technical colleges developed courses for full professional qualifications in engineering and commerce and, in some cases,

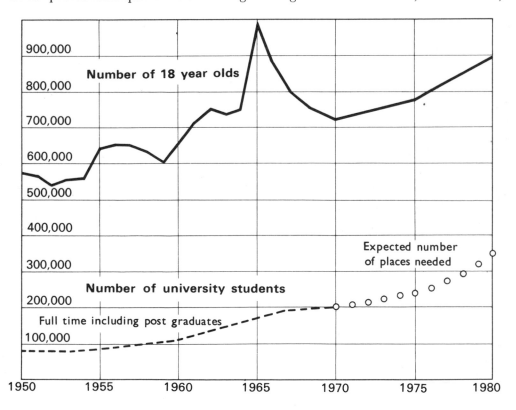

35 The rising number of university students is the result of two factors: the increasing proportion of young people who want to attend university and can reach the required standards and the rising number of people of university age in the population. When relating the two curves in this chart to one another it should be remembered that the university population consists of other age groups besides 18-year-olds.

for external degrees of London University. Originally these institutions had provided training for working-class boys and in many cases had developed from the Mechanics' Institutes of the nineteenth century. Generally, technical college courses catered for students unable to afford a university course and were developed particularly in large towns such as London, Bradford and Manchester.

In 1944 the Education Act brought technical education under the control of the Ministry of Education and its provision became the duty of local education authorities. Shortly after the passing of the Act an event occurred which promoted the growth of advanced work in some technical colleges.

After the end of the War a scheme of students' grants for discharged ex-servicemen was introduced. The demand from ex-servicemen was mainly for courses in the applied sciences and technology. As the universities were unable to cope the Government allowed grants to be used for places on degree and other courses in technical colleges. This policy encouraged not only the expansion of existing facilities in colleges such as Battersea Polytechnic and the Royal Technical College, Salford but also the growth of degree courses in colleges such as Acton Technical College which previously had not attempted work at this level. The colleges which expanded or introduced work of a university standard were among those which, a decade later, were to be the institutions forming the new technological universities.

For a period of fifteen years or so after the War the Government regarded the growth of higher education in the technical colleges as a temporary measure. It was hoped that in due course the universities would be able to meet the demand for places. Thus the fifties tended to be a period of disillusionment for the leading technical colleges. Having experienced the status of university work they were now faced with a future in which it was to be taken from them.

36 Cambridge, 1939. Academic life at the universities continued throughout the war, but afterwards they were unable to meet the increased demand for scientific and technical education. This led to the expansion of the technical colleges.

However in the mid-fifties the scale of technical development in such countries as the USA and the USSR, and the number of technologists and technicians being trained by these countries caused growing unease among politicians. By 1956 the position seemed so critical that urgent action was considered necessary. A White Paper on Technical Education issued in that year put forward far-reaching plans. At the same time, a grim picture was drawn of the existing position. Two examples will suffice. First, only about half of students who completed advanced courses in technical colleges became technologists. Secondly, there were insufficient numbers of girls and women seeking technical training. ('Their hopes are naturally bent on marriage and they fear perhaps – though there is much experience to prove them wrong – that by aiming at a certificate they may miss a husband.') The White Paper considered that technical education could not be improved by part-time day release and evening classes. It considered 'advanced sandwich courses would therefore probably become the main avenue of progress towards the highest technological qualifications'.

The major emphasis in the White Paper had been the need for more technologists. The Government responded in two ways. First, in June 1956 it was announced that development of advanced technological work was to be concentrated in eight colleges – the colleges of advanced technology – soon to be known as CATS. The colleges selected were the Royal Technical College at Salford, the Bradford Institute of Technology, the Loughborough College of Technology, Birmingham and Cardiff Colleges of Technology, and, in London, the Battersea, Chelsea, and Northampton Polytechnics. In September 1960 the Bristol College of Technology was added to the list and the Brunel College of Technology was designated in 1962.

37 The University of Bath was formed from a College of Advanced Technology. It offers a wide range of studies with a technical and scientific bias. The illustrations shows the School of Biological Sciences with the Open Air Theatre in the right foreground.

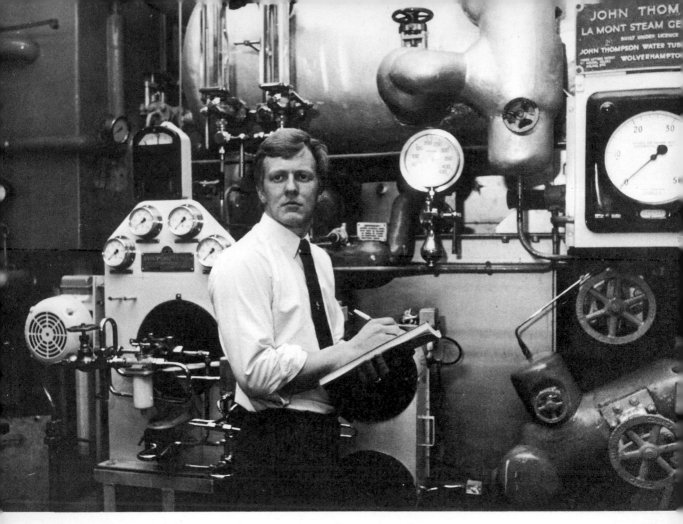

38 The University of Aston was formerly Birmingham College of Advanced Technology. This student in the mechanical engineering workshop is on a sandwich course.

The decision called for far-reaching changes in the colleges. They were expected to transform themselves from localised colleges into institutions drawing students from all areas of the country and concentrating on university-level work. Elementary work was to be quickly dispensed with. Secondly, the National Council for Technological Awards was created. The Council was set up to make awards to students on completion of authorised courses in authorised colleges. Both the course and the award were to be of honours degree standard but because of objections raised by the universities, the award was called not a degree but a diploma – the Diploma of Technology.

The course for a Dip.Tech. (as it was familiarly known) was a combination of industrial training and academic education. This characteristic distinguished it from a university degree and also lengthened the course to four years. Training for the Dip.Tech. was carried out by 'sandwich' courses, the usual pattern being six months in a college and six months in industry alternately. The industrial training provided practical experience and the opportunity to work with equipment on a scale that could not be provided in the college. It also gave experience of working under economic and production conditions which could not be reproduced in the college. These sandwich courses are comparable in some ways with the medical students' training and have been described as 'walking the wards of industry'.

Before the NCTA was set up, the degree level work of the technical colleges was aimed at external degrees of the University of London. Permission to offer courses for London degrees had to be obtained from the University. This requirement was usually a formality and approval was sometimes given to degree courses in colleges where facilities were inadequate. The NCTA was set up as an inspecting and supervising body and it set new standards in accommodation, course requirements and staffing. If colleges were judged to be inadequate in any of these respects, the Council denied them recognition. On the other hand, the colleges received a good deal of freedom under the NCTA being given the responsibility of drawing up curricula and of conducting examinations.

After its establishment the Dip.Tech. became widely recognised and the universities played a leading part in its success. For instance, the Committee of Vice-Chancellors recommended the acceptance of the honours Dip.Tech. as equivalent to an honours degree in admitting students to university courses for postgraduate qualifications. Industry also played a part by recognition and active support. Leading industrial firms not only recognised the Dip.Tech. as the equivalent of a B.Sc., but, in some cases, demonstrated a marked preference for Dip.Tech. holders rather than university graduates.

Such was the widespread recognition achieved by the Dip.Tech. that a proposal in 1963 to replace it by a bachelor's degree drew little protest from the universities. At the same time the NCTA was converted into the Council for National Academic Awards (CNAA) and given a royal charter to grant degrees for courses in all fields of study and by all patterns of study. The latter phrase refers to part-time, sandwich and full-time courses. The original NCTA formula of inspection and supervision of curricula and general facilities has been retained. Rather like London University in its early days, the CNAA is really an examining University. It awards degrees to students who pursue their higher education in establishments for further education which do not have the power to award their own degrees.

After their designation from 1956–1957 onwards the Colleges of Advanced Technology made remarkable progress. In the session 1962–1963 over 90 per cent of the full-time students were taking advanced courses, that is, courses beyond the Advanced level of the General Certificate of Education or its equivalent. As planned, a great deal of lower level work had been shed. The number of advanced full-time students grew from 4,700 in 1956–1957 to 10,300 in 1962–1963.

The Robbins Committee on Higher Education, reporting in 1963, found that the powers and status of the colleges were not in line with the work they performed. In particular, the CATs were not empowered to award their own degrees despite

55

the fact that their curricula, staffing and facilities were approved by the NCTA for honours degree work. The Report pointed out that the new university foundations had awarded degrees from the beginning, whereas in contrast, the CATS (many of which had a long history), were 'kept in a position of tutelage so that they are less attractive to students and their recruitment of staff is impeded'. The Report went on to recommend that the CATS should become technological universities with the right to grant their own degrees. Their status was to become equivalent to that of existing universities.

Following the Robbins Report, all the CATS except Chelsea, which was absorbed into the University of London, received charters as independent universities. Only two of them have retained the technological label in their titles – Bath University of Technology (formerly the Bristol College of Technology) and Loughborough University of Technology. The Bradford Institute of Technology has become the University of Bradford, Northampton College of Advanced Technology has become the City University, Battersea College of Technology has become the University of Surrey and has moved to Guildford, Brunel College has moved ten miles (16 km) away from Acton to a larger site near Uxbridge as Brunel University. The others have become the University of Salford, the University of Aston, and the Cardiff Institute of Science and Technology which is affiliated to the University of Wales.

Since the acquisition of university status the technological universities have made very definite efforts to widen their academic scope. Departments have been started in arts or general studies, in social studies, in economics, business management and sociology. While the distinctive scientific and technological flavour will, doubtless, be maintained for a long time, it seems certain that the differences between the former CATS and the older civic universities will eventually be considerably reduced.

New Foundations

Seven new universities were set up in the sixties. The University of Sussex opened in 1961 and was followed by East Anglia and York (1963), Essex and Lancaster (1964), Warwick and Kent (1965). A comparison between their foundation and that of the nineteenth century civic universities indicates a number of interesting differences.

The nineteenth century foundations were the product of local initiative; the new universities are the planned results of Government policy. The Government decided that so many universities ought to be created and it promoted their foundation whereas formerly it merely assessed an applicant institution to test its suitability.

All the provincial universities were financed by funds raised locally in the form of either private donations or public subscription, before they received any Government help. The new foundations in the sixties received Government aid from the start.

Starting with Owens College in Manchester in 1851, all the provincial universities had their origin in university colleges whose students read for London external degrees. This system provided a period of apprenticeship which enabled the colleges to draw up their own curriculum and, in due course, to grant their own degrees. The new universities on the other hand, received their charters at their foundation without passing through a period of apprenticeship. Furthermore they granted their own degrees from the start.

The 'atmosphere' of the new universities is quite different from that of the early years of the civic universities. Instead of congested sites in the centre of industrial cities, the new universities enjoy spacious 'green field' sites and more buildings. From the start they have aimed at non-local students and have experimented with new courses and teaching methods.

FURTHER READING

M. Beloff, *The Plateglass Universities* Secker and Warburg

M. Argles, *South Kensington to Robbins: An Account of Technical and Scientific Education since 1851* Longmans

6 Organisation and Finance

University Officers

Universities are self-governing bodies which derive their rights from Royal Charters.

At the head of a university is the *Chancellor*. The person elected to this office is generally a nationally known figure – perhaps a member of the Royal Family or a former cabinet minister. Such a person has interests outside of the university and is unable to give much time to its day-to-day administration. Generally, the Chancellor appears only on ceremonial occasions such as presentation of degrees.

The officer in charge of the academic and administrative arrangements of a modern university is called the *Vice-Chancellor*. For all practical purposes he is the head of the university. At most British universities the Vice-Chancellor holds office until retirement age is reached, but at universities such as Oxford, Cambridge and London which are made up of a number of colleges, the principals of the various colleges hold the office in turn for short periods.

The *Registrar* and the *Bursar* share responsibility for the administration of the university. The Bursar deals with financial matters whereas the Registrar is

39 The procession to Encaenia in Oxford, 1904. The Chancellor, Viscount Goschen, leads the new doctors, who include the Archbishop of Canterbury.

40 A Vice-Chancellor is, for all practical purposes, the head of a university. Dr J. A. Pope is Vice-Chancellor of the University of Aston in Birmingham. He is shown standing in front of the Sports Hall which features a climbing wall on one of the outside walls.

concerned with academic matters. Correspondence and queries on most problems, including admission, are usually addressed to the Registrar.

University Government

The usual pattern of government in a university comprises Court, Council and Senate. The supreme governing body of a university is usually called the *Court*. It may be a very large body with up to several hundred members. Meetings are held several times a year and reports are received on the progress of the university. Although the Court is, as already stated, the highest governing body, it does not meet often enough to enable its members to exercise real control. It has been likened to a court of appeal in that it is useful if any particularly difficult problems arise. The people appointed to membership of the Court – representatives of other universities, of local authorities, of industry and commerce, of graduates and of students – often have expert knowledge which may be valuable to the university.

The *Council* acts as the executive committee of a university and is responsible for its financial affairs. It consists of a smaller group of people than the Court and includes in its membership representatives of the academic staff of the university and successful businessmen. The latter have experience of controlling large sums of money in their work and this experience is invaluable whenever financial matters are under discussion.

Like the older universities, the new English universities of the 1960s have Courts with large memberships. However, very few have retained the Court as the supreme governing body and it has been largely replaced by the Council as the ultimate governing authority.

The *Senate* is the chief academic body and consists mainly of university teachers. Usually its members include the heads of departments, the university librarian and others who have a powerful voice in university affairs. The Senate is responsible, through its sub-committees, for the appointment of teaching staff and for

41 The formal structure of the University of Bath as projected in 1965. The organisation is typical of the patterns of university government.

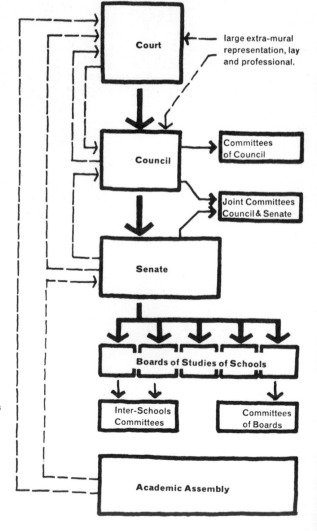

Initially about 75 members, growing eventually to 300 or 400.
Chancellor as Chairman.
The ultimate governing body of the University.

large extra-mural representation, lay and professional.

35 members, lay majority.
Elected Chairman.
Responsible for non-academic management and general financial policy.

40-45 members, all academic.
Vice-Chancellor as Chairman.
Responsible for overall academic policy.

25-30 members each.
Heads of Schools as Chairmen.
Responsible for general and academic management of each School.

Formed as required to investigate new courses and joint research projects.

All academic staff.
Elected Chairman.
Can make recommendations to Council and Senate.

Court

Council

Committees of Council

Joint Committees Council & Senate

Senate

Boards of Studies of Schools

Inter-Schools Committees

Committees of Boards

Academic Assembly

42 The Senate is the chief academic body of a university. The illustration shows a meeting of the Senate of the University of Newcastle-upon-Tyne.

promoting any changes of an academic nature. Its chairman is the Vice-Chancellor who, in addition, is always a member of the Council, and so serves as a useful link between the two bodies.

Organisation of Courses

Universities organise their academic work in a variety of ways. In the older universities, subjects are taught in individual *departments* which are in turn grouped into *faculties*. The latter cover the broad subject groupings such as arts, science, engineering and social science. Law, education, theology, and medicine usually form faculties of their own. A committee called a *Faculty Board* governs each faculty. Each Faculty has a *Dean*, elected by members of that Faculty. The Dean acts as chairman at meetings of the Faculty and, in addition, in some universities, is responsible for the admission of students.

A Faculty is sub-divided into departments. Although the work of the departments is overseen by the Faculty, in many instances the departments have a high degree of autonomy.

In the universities founded after 1945, the traditional faculty structure has been avoided in an attempt to encourage students to study across the accepted subject boundaries. One form of organisation, pioneered by Sussex, is the 'school'. The latter embraces a range of related subjects but at the same time they are studied in relation to a particular theme, such as English and European studies; African and Asian studies; social studies.

Teaching methods vary from university to university and within many universities, from department to department. Teaching takes three principal forms, namely, lectures, seminars and tutorials (see Chapter 8).

Degrees

A degree is the title conferred by a university as a recognition of scholarship. The original meaning of 'degree' was that of a step or stage by which the student progressed to his mastership and doctorate. In medieval times the degree was a certificate of fitness to teach at a university although in some universities the recognition as master was a two-sided matter. In the first place, the licence to teach was conferred as an academic hallmark by the Chancellor of the university. Secondly the young master had to be accepted into the fellowship of existing masters by the ceremony of 'inception'.

Until fairly recent times, degrees have been awarded as a result of examination by oral disputation, that is, argument between the candidate and the examiner. Evidence of this is to be found in names still used for the examinations at the older universities. For example, in Oxford the entrance examination is called 'Responsions'; in Cambridge a top place in the mathematical tripos for the year goes to a 'Wrangler'. But oral examining was an inexact way of assessing proficiency and as the universities grew larger it had a bad effect on the standard of scholarship. The notorious abuses of the oral system during the eighteenth century were described in Chapter 1. Thus in the late eighteenth and early nineteenth centuries searching written examinations were introduced into Oxford and Cambridge.

The present-day degree system tends to be rather confusing. Only careful study of a university's degree structure can indicate what a particular qualification means in terms of length of study and standard of achievement.

Generally degrees can be classified into first degrees and higher degrees.

A first degree is the qualification normally awarded to an undergraduate after successfully completing his course. It is usually called a bachelor's degree and it may be awarded in Arts (B.A.) or Science (B.Sc.). There are, however, a number of others, such as LL.B. (Law) and B.Mus. (Music). At Oxford, Cambridge and Keele, all first degrees are B.A. degrees, regardless of subject.

For first degrees a minimum period of three or four years' residence at the university is necessary. The only exceptions are for London University external degrees for which there are no conditions of residence or attendance at lectures. Certain courses leading to professional qualifications are longer than four years. For example, courses in medicine and dentistry may be as long as six years.

There are two kinds of first degree, namely, a pass, ordinary or general degree and an honours or special degree. For a pass degree a student studies a number of subjects whereas for an honours degree, one subject is studied in depth. An honours degree is normally judged to be of higher academic standard than a pass degree. Successful candidates at the final honours examination are divided into class I, II and III. Unsuccessful candidates may be given a pass degree. A uniform standard of degree throughout the country is ensured by having external examiners on all university examining boards.

There are three categories of higher degrees, namely, masterships, doctorates in philosophy and senior doctorates. Various conditions have to be fulfilled for these

43 His Royal Highness the Duke of Edinburgh, Chancellor of the University of Salford, awards her degree to the first woman graduate in Mechanical Engineering, in December 1969.

higher degrees but one common requirement is that the candidate must already have a first degree.

Usually masters' degrees are awarded as a result of study beyond the first degree stage, but at Oxford and Cambridge the Master of Arts (M.A.) degree is given after a certain period of time has elapsed and on payment of a fee. To make the situation even more confusing, the M.A. is the first degree in arts subjects at all Scottish universities.

The Doctor of Philosophy degree (Ph.D. or D.Phil.) can be obtained in a wide variety of subjects. It is by no means confined to philosophy itself. The degree is usually conferred after submission of a thesis giving an account of research work.

Senior doctorates such as Doctor of Literature (D.Lit.) or Doctor of Science (D.Sc.) are awarded on the merits of published material which represents the results of original research and scholarship.

Degree presentation is an elaborate ceremony at many universities. Members of the university wear academic dress. Graduates wear gowns and hoods of a distinctive colour varying with the university and with the degree the graduate has passed.

Finance

Money for the maintenance and development of universities comes from three sources, namely, fees paid by students, donations from private sources (such as endowments and gifts from business firms) and grants from the State. These three sources of finance have all been used in the past and all play some part today, but grants from the State have become completely dominant.

State financial interest in the universities has developed over a long period. Grants were made to the Scottish universities from the time of the Union in 1707; London also received grants from its earliest years, specifically towards the cost of examinations; and early grants were made to the Welsh university colleges. In 1889 a more formal system came into existence.

In their early stages the civic universities founded during the nineteenth century (see Chapter 3) were handicapped by lack of funds. Despite this they survived through the generosity of local benefactors. However funds from private sources eventually became almost exhausted and in 1889 the House of Commons voted the sum of £15,000 per year to be distributed among the university colleges. The condition of the grant was that each institution should perform 'an appreciable amount of advanced university work.' This was interpreted to mean the provision for post-graduate research work as well as of courses for undergraduates.

The annual grant was distributed initially on the advice of a series of *ad hoc* committees. After a time a more permanent committee was established and in July 1919 a body known as the *University Grants Committee* was established. The Committee received a block grant from the Treasury and allocated it among the universities. The present-day UGC continues to fulfil this task and its functions are to assess the needs of the universities, to seek the necessary finances from the Government, and then to allocate sums of money to each university for a five-year period.

The majority of the members of the Committee are on a staff of a university while the remainder are representative of industry and commerce. Members of the Committee visit the universities to discuss their financial needs and plans for development. The grant covers expenditure on current expenses and also capital expenditure for building work.

From its beginning, the Committee has respected the control of each university over its internal affairs. A university is free to decide what it will teach, the details of its syllabuses and the organisation of its own examinations for degrees and diplomas. The universities are not under the control of the Department of Education or indeed of any other Government Department. This freedom from State control has been due largely to the existence of the UGC. It acts as a link between the Government and the universities.

In 1919–1920 grants from the Treasury amounted to £692,000 and formed 28.8 per cent of the universities' total income. By 1938–1939 the grant income had grown to £2,079,000 but the proportion to total income was only a little higher at 31 per cent. Today the position is very different. The contributions of the

Government through the UGC amount now to about 80 per cent of the total income of the universities. In 1970–1971 the total Government grant came to approximately £241 million.

In spite of the large sums of public money spent on universities they have remained autonomous institutions. However, there are increasing pressures to put an end to this independence. For example, the Robbins Committee in their Report on Higher Education (1963) argued that the Minister of Education should be responsible to Parliament for the whole of the educational system. The Committee considered that the separation of the universities, in the administrative sense, from the schools which provide them with students, was not helpful to good planning or co-ordination. How far the autonomy of the universities can be balanced with their growing dependence on State aid is a problem that will loom large in the future.

FURTHER READING
S. Caine, *British Universities: Purpose and Prospects* Bodley Head
G. L. Brook, *The Modern University* Deutsch
Report of Committee on Higher Education 1963 (Robbins Report) H.M.S.O.

7 Students

The medieval university student was, according to Professor G. M. Trevelyan, 'riotous, lawless and licentious'. In addition he was 'miserably poor' and being unable to afford books, he learned very little. Very often he left the university without taking a degree.

In some respects discipline in the colleges became too strict in the fifteenth and sixteenth centuries. At least this must have been so if all the college rules were enforced. However it is always difficult to know how far and how often the rules were enforced, and presumably matters adjusted themselves to circumstances and cases. At any rate the time had passed when there was no such thing as academic discipline.

When a sixteenth century student entered the university he or his parents contracted privately with one of the fellows of a college to act both as teacher and guardian. Each private tutor had about half a dozen students whom he taught and the relationship was similar to that of master and apprentice.

On the whole this system of private tutoring worked well but there was a tendency for the tutor to neglect those of his students who did not pay high fees. On the other hand, he was indulgent to the richer students.

By the eighteenth and nineteenth centuries many young men from wealthy families went to the university because it was the custom – rather than from any wish to obtain a degree. They lived extravagantly, waited on by their own servants or by the poorer students.

University regulations were again tightened towards the end of the nineteenth century and the life of the twentieth century student is very different from that of his predecessors. At Oxford and Cambridge each student lives in college and

44 The Prince of Wales, Albert Edward, attended Oxford in 1859–60. He did not mix with the students and had his own tutors. He had a select group of friends at Christ Church, some of whom are seen with him (*seated, centre*) in this cricket team.

45 *(above)* The Refectory at the University of Sussex.

46 *(below)* Most modern student halls have study/bedrooms like this one in Lawrence Tower, University of Aston. Here students have their own front door keys, individual bedrooms, and shared amenity rooms for cooking, laundry, etc.

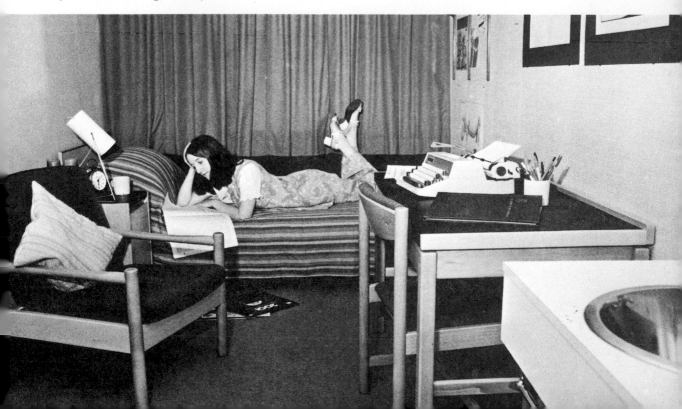

has a room or two rooms of his own. Most of his meals are taken in Hall, that is in the college dining hall. The fellows and tutors of the college dine at high table, usually on a dais at the upper end of the hall. Undergraduates dine at the other tables.

The proportion of students that other universities can house varies considerably. Generally, the aim is to make accommodation available for up to about 60 per cent, although at present between 40 and 50 per cent is a more usual figure. In the past, universities have housed their students in halls of residence but this form of community life (with wardens to watch over the students) is giving way to alternative forms of accommodation. These include purpose-built blocks of student flats and converted student houses for small groups. The advantage over the traditional hall of residence is that students are given a greater measure of freedom. In addition, these forms of accommodation are much cheaper to finance than the rather grandiose halls of residence.

Student Organisation

At many universities, student life centres on the Student Union to which all students automatically belong. The Union, which is sometimes called a guild of undergraduates, is a loose federation of all the students at the university. Subscriptions are included in the fees paid on behalf of the student by the local authority which provides the maintenance grant. Each subscription can be as much as £16 per student and consequently a union can have an income running well into five figures.

The Student Union is governed by the Union Council. Election to it is arranged on a 'constituency' basis with the constituency based on the departmental or school organisation of the university. Senior officers of the Union are elected by the whole student body. The hard work involved in running the Union is such that student presidents are often allowed a year of leave from their studies during their term of office.

In addition to elections, the student body as a whole can usually express its views in regular general meetings. In theory, at least, the Union officers are responsible to the general meeting and must obey its decisions. However, for the system to be successful, a majority of the students must take an active part and this is difficult to achieve.

Student Unions are providing an increasing range of services for their members. These facilities range from student concessions in local shops (usually in the form of discounts) to cheap travel arrangements, insurance, shops (for example, selling second hand books) and an employment agency for vacation work. In addition, the work of a Union is taken up with organising student social life, administering Union buildings, taking a hand in the problems of student welfare and housing, and organising student social work. Not surprisingly, most Unions employ a number of clerical staff and the larger ones have full-time managers to run what is in effect a large business.

47   The Oxford Union is famous for debates. This is the Committee of the Union in 1895.

Membership of the Student Union at the university automatically carries with it membership of the National Union of Students. The NUS acts as the voice of student opinion throughout the country. Twice yearly a National Council of Students is held and matters of importance to the student community are discussed. Many services are provided for students by the NUS, including continental holidays and cheap student charter flights to European cities. In addition a student with a problem such as, for example, an inadequate maintenance grant, can contact the local NUS representative and an attempt will be made to provide a solution.

Student Social Life

In most universities, social amenities are provided in a separate Union building. Facilities range from the luxurious (bars, lounges, colour television, overnight accommodation, a ballroom, council and debating chambers, snack bars and restaurants, shops, laundrettes, and libraries) to the rather cramped and over-crowded conditions found in some fast-growing universities.

Some universities have experimented successfully with a central social building

69

for both students and the teaching staff. Elsewhere the staff and students prefer to have separate social amenities.

Organised student social life is generally catered for by the Union. Visits from both the popular and less well-known 'pop' groups have, to a large extent, replaced the traditional weekly Saturday night dances (known as 'hops') and transformed the balls which remain the highlights of the Union year.

The various student societies are supervised and financed by the Union. Drama, folk-song and classical music societies seem to be consistently popular, while university orchestras and choirs frequently reach very high standards of performance. Debating and politics are less popular than they used to be although students still use these clubs as training grounds for future political careers. Various religious groups flourish and so does the social work carried out by students in the locality of the university. This under-publicised activity includes work with the old and under-privileged and patients in hospitals. It is of interest to note here that in some universities the traditional rather riotous rag week is being replaced by a programme of social work. Where rag weeks are still held, the proceeds are now often used to finance charitable work run by the students themselves. Formerly the proceeds were simply handed over to outside charities.

Many of the popular societies reflect the hobbies of students and radio, chess, bridge and photography remain ever-popular. New societies are constantly being introduced. If someone arrives at the university with a keen interest, and can find one or two like-minded fellow students, then a society has been born.

Another opening for talent is provided by the student newspaper. In universities where there are local radio stations, students are also writing and producing regular programmes from the campus.

In almost all cases, the universities provide exceptional sports facilities, and sport plays an important part in university life. Undergraduates who represent their university in major national games or sports are awarded their university colours. Probably the best known of these are the dark blue of Oxford, the light blue of Cambridge and the purple of London. For the minor sports such as boxing,

49 Rowing and rugby are amongst the best-known of the universities' many sporting activities. This is Eights Week at Oxford.

fencing or lacrosse, a half-blue or its equivalent is awarded. Many universities have appointed directors of physical education who are responsible not only for coaching university teams, but also provide teaching in many sports from the most elementary level. Student sports clubs are often organised by a separate athletics union and not by the main students union. The work involved is sufficient to justify the existence of a separate organisation. At national level sports competitions between the universities are organised by the Universities Athletic Union and the British Universities Sports Federation. The UAU is responsible for team and individual championships while the BUSF organises representative and international matches for British university teams.

Student Welfare

The general pattern is to assign each student to a member of the university academic staff. The tutor is generally responsible for keeping a watchful eye on his students' progress, and his advice is available on academic and personal problems. Non-academic problems are, however, increasingly the concern of a university's health service. Most health services are staffed with at least one full-time physician and nursing staff. Student counselling services are also available.

Most universities have appointments services which provide advice on careers and put undergraduates in touch with prospective employers. In addition, arrangements are made for employers to visit the university and interview candidates.

Admission

In the Middle Ages, anyone who was not debarred for religious reasons and who had sufficient money, reasonable health, and a desire to study, could write his name on the roll of a Master at a university and attend lectures. Students had to

71

find enough money to pay the lecturers' fees, the expense of food and clothes and to support themselves in lodgings or in hostels. This system continued until Oxford and Cambridge introduced entrance examinations in the nineteenth century. The other universities followed their example.

The present-day system of admission to the universities is by examination and selection. There is no religious test and women are admitted on equal terms with men for most subjects. General Certificate of Education results provide an indication of a candidate's ability and the universities use them to select students for admission. There are two sets of entrance requirements, namely, general and course requirements.

The general requirement is set by the university and is designed to ensure that undergraduates have had a wide and broadly-based education. Apart from English, individual subjects are not usually mentioned and the general requirement is expressed, therefore, as a certain number of passes in GCE Ordinary and Advanced level, with no mention of grades. For example, passes in five approved subjects at 'O' and 'A' level, including at least two passes at 'A' level may be required. An alternative pattern is passes in four approved subjects at 'O' and 'A' level, including three subjects at 'A' level. Most universities accept either of these two patterns of entrance requirements.

The course requirement is more complicated. In this case the department or faculty responsible for the course of study names the subject which the teaching staff consider candidates should have studied before they can take the course. For example, mathematics is, very often, a course requirement for the sciences and economics. It is very likely that some departments may ask for more 'A' level passes than the number laid down in the general requirements of their university.

Examination results are not the only means of selection for a university. School reports and students' own accounts of their outside interests play an important part, as may a candidate's performance at interview. At one time, candidates applied directly to a university for admission. However the enormous increase in recent years in the number of applications has resulted in the development of a new application procedure. Prospective candidates for nearly all the universities apply for places through the Universities Central Council on Admissions (UCCA). The only students who apply directly are applicants to the Open University and Scottish candidates for the Universities of Glasgow, Aberdeen, Strathclyde and Dundee.

Discipline

At most universities the penalty for a severe breach of discipline, or for failure to pass an important examination is to be 'sent down' (expulsion) or to be 'rusticated' (temporarily suspended). At Oxford and Cambridge the proctors have, for many centuries, been responsible for maintaining discipline. Proctors are officers of the university elected from among their own fellows by the Colleges. Each evening the proctors clad in cap and gown accompanied by their constables

50 The 'Gown and Town Row' was a regular feature of Oxford life when hostility between the local people and the students erupted into violence. On this occasion, 5 November, 1815, both fireworks and blows were exchanged.

or 'bulldogs' patrol the town. The university is anxious that the conduct of its members does not interfere with the peace of the townspeople and the proctors' nightly walks are an expression of that concern. An undergraduate who is found breaking regulations is summoned next morning to the proctors and probably fined.

Student Representation

The representation of students on the various governing bodies and committees of the universities is increasing steadily. This is particularly noticeable on committees which are concerned with matters directly affecting students, such as welfare, accommodation etc.

As was noted in the last chapter, the Court is the supreme governing body but it meets only once a year and is far too unwieldy to do any detailed work. The really powerful governing bodies are the Council and the Senate and it is on these bodies that students have concentrated their efforts to achieve representation. Some universities have worked out a formula which provides representation without giving students actual membership of Council or Senate. This has been achieved by forming new general committees of both bodies consisting of all the normal members plus student representatives. In this way, matters such as academic appointments or the records of individual students can be allowed for by making them the sole concern of the Council or Senate.

In most universities, departmental, school and faculty staff and student committees have been set up in order to work out ways for student involvement in academic affairs at this level.

One problem of representation which, perhaps, students had not expected to face, is the number of seats on university bodies which they are required to fill. In some universities the figure can be up to 60 seats and general student apathy is such that it is not always easy to fill them.

FURTHER READING
G. L. Brook, *The Modern University* Andre Deutsch

8 The Work of a University

The work of a university can be divided into three main parts: the teaching of undergraduates; research; and service to the general public.

Undergraduate Teaching

Instruction is by lectures, tutorials, seminars, and in certain subjects through practical work in laboratories.

Lectures are given to large groups of students and the aim of the lecturer is to provide direction and guidance in students' studies.

A tutorial is a method of teaching in which the tutor devotes a period each week to the tuition of one or two students. A tutorial differs from a lecture in that the starting-point is the student's own ideas (often in the form of an essay) which the tutor subjects to critical examination. The personal relationship established by the tutorial gives the tutor a thorough knowledge of the merits and shortcomings of his undergraduates. Hence a tutor's report is generally valued by a prospective employer.

Discussion groups or seminars are useful because they encourage students to take an active part in the process of learning.

A library is an essential part of a university and to learn how to use books effectively is a vital part of a student's education. The strength of a university's library is, therefore, important to undergraduates and the riches of their libraries form an important part of the attraction of Oxford and Cambridge. The two older universities each have libraries containing more than two million volumes. Of the more modern universities, London is in a unique position in having the British Museum Library within easy reach. The University of Manchester benefits by

51 Medieval students around their teacher (from the *Canterbury Psalter*).

52 A lecture at Exeter University.

having the John Rylands Library in the same city; and students at the University College of Wales at Aberystwyth have access to the National Library of Wales. Other universities are building up collections of rare books. These special collections are a great asset to a university library in that they provide facilities for research and attract scholars from all over the world. Generally, however, they are not of much use to undergraduates whose main need is a collection of standard text books.

To what extent should a university train undergraduates for particular jobs? Some degree of controversy surrounds this matter of vocational training.

At present, it is exceptional for a university degree to be sufficient by itself to obtain a professional qualification. However, his degree often entitles a graduate to *some* exemption from professional training. For example, in the legal profession, the rules of the London Inns of Court and of the English Law Society provide for reduction of the period of training for barristers or solicitors who hold degrees. Exemption from part of the examinations for those who have taken law in their degrees is also granted. Similarly, the Institutes of Chartered Accountants in England and Wales and in Scotland grant a reduction in the minimum period of articles for United Kingdom graduates. Holders of 'approved degrees' are granted exemption from the intermediate stage of the accountancy examination.

53 Corpus Christi College Library, Cambridge.

Normally it is possible for a professional qualification such as accountancy, banking or surveying to be obtained without following a university course. Medicine is the exception and attendance at a university is part of the process of qualification. In this profession, therefore, the universities have completely re-established the predominance which they enjoyed in the Middle Ages. The old established and highly reputed medical schools attached to leading hospitals have all come into the university world. Probably the most important event in this connection was the incorporation of the London hospital medical schools in the University of London in 1900.

Thus, with the exception of medicine the universities play only a part and often a minor part, in present-day education for the professions. The universities supply a general training but the specialized knowledge and experience demanded by most professions has to be acquired after completion of the university course.

Research

In addition to the teaching of undergraduates, a university is concerned with research or the discovery of new knowledge. It has not always been so. For example,

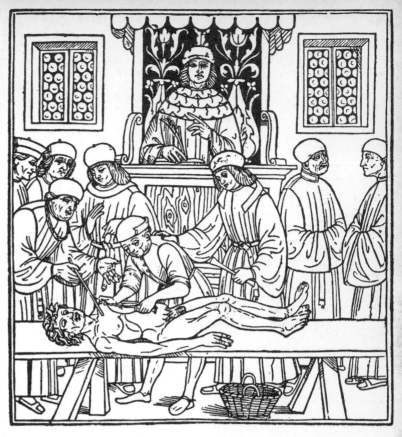

54 Medicine is one of the few professions for which universities have provided training, and this has been an important function since Medieval times.

over a century ago, in his various publications on universities, Cardinal Newman considered that research was not the business of a university. He declared that research ought to be undertaken by separate 'academies' while the university concentrated on teaching undergraduates. Up to the time when Newman wrote, the universities had done very little research.

Nevertheless, university opinion was slowly turning to a belief in the value of research. Thus in 1874 the Cavendish Laboratory was built at Cambridge and eventually became one of the great world centres for the development of physical science. John Stuart Mill was almost the last outstanding economist with no university post. After him came W. S. Jevons, Alfred Marshall and a succession of other university professors. A similar development took place in history. David Hume, William Robertson, Edward Gibbon and Lord Macauley worked outside the universities, but in the twentieth century the great historians – G. M. Trevelyan, R. H. Tawney, A. J. Toynbee, A. J. P. Taylor, to mention only a few, are to be found within the universities.

Why have researchers in modern times been attracted to the universities?

In the first place, the university of today offers all kinds of essential facilities for research. Laboratories and expensive equipment are available to the chemist and the physicist; and extensive libraries are at the disposal of researchers in the arts subjects. Research in the social sciences very often involves an extensive use of statistics and the availability of university computers is a great help in this respect. In addition, the secretarial and typing facilities provided for university staff and

55 Until the late nineteenth century the universities did not concern themselves very much with research. Most of the well-known original thinkers in the seventeenth and eighteenth centuries had attended a university and some held university appointments, but these connections contributed very little to their thinking. The political and economic thinkers—Jeremy Bentham, David Ricardo, T. R. Malthus, James Mill and John Stuart Mill, and the initiators of the theory of evolution Charles Darwin (shown here) and Alfred Russell Wallace—never held university posts. Neither did Karl Marx, whose writings have been so influential in economics and politics.

the research grants which may be made available from university funds are further attractions.

A second factor is the opportunities offered by a university of contact with other researchers. Experts in a great many subjects are found on the staff of a university and, in addition, a university post offers the possibility of contacts with specialists who hold posts at other universities.

There are, therefore, great attractions in a modern university for people who wish to carry out research. Today the universities are among the principal centres of research and it is taken for granted that they must be as concerned with the discovery of new knowledge as with teaching undergraduates.

Service to the general public

In addition to teaching internal students and carrying our research, universities play an important role in the general cultural life of the community. There are a number of ways in which universities provide for the intellectual and cultural needs of the general public. They include extramural work, public lectures, encouragement of the arts, broadcasting and publishing.

'Extramural' means activities arranged outside of a university. Extramural work began when the universities of Cambridge, London and Oxford provided extension courses in the second half of the nineteenth century. At that time there was no Government financial help and attendance at extension classes tended to be confined to those who could afford to pay the tuition fees. Finance from the Board of Education for extension work became available from 1908 onwards and in 1919 there was an official recommendation that the universities

56 The universities of the eighteenth century made no attempt to teach in the field of technology. It was only to be expected, therefore, that the inventions associated with the Industrial Revolution came from mechanics or inventors and not from university scholars. Examples of these technological developments were the work of James Watt on steam engines, the spinning machine of Richard Arkwright and the steam locomotive of George Stephenson, seen here teaching navvies.

should establish extramural departments. By the 1930s most universities had a Department of Extramural Studies or of Adult Education.

Members of the public who join extramural courses come from all sections of the population. The most popular subjects are social studies, archaeology and history, English language and literature, the visual arts, and music.

In addition to these general courses, most departments arrange refresher courses of some kind, such as courses for married women wishing to return to their professions after bringing up families. Provision is also made for day-time courses for special groups of people such as industrial managers, clergymen, magistrates, probation officers, lawyers and prison officers.

An important development has been provision of courses for London external degree students. These courses are particularly intended for those relying on correspondence courses. Since the Cambridge Extramural Department held the first residential course of this nature in 1962–1963, similar courses have been held elsewhere.

Although many extramural classes still meet in drab and uncomfortable school classrooms, an increasing number of departments now have purpose-built centres. Facilities often include a library, common rooms, a stage, and lecture and discussion rooms. Some departments also have their own residential centres.

Public lectures are another form of public service. This type of lecture is open equally to the public and to members of the university. Public lectures in this sense are a traditional feature of university life and most universities make arrangements for them. Occasionally these lectures are badly supported but generally they are well attended with the size of the audience numbering several hundred people. A public lecture serves to bring the leading scholars of the day into the university and to introduce them to a large number of people. Quite often, the lectures are reported in some detail in the press or published as a book or pamphlet. For example, the Annual Oration at the London School of Economics is always published as a pamphlet.

Another sphere of university service activity is in the arts, and includes music and drama as well as the visual arts. Some universities have permanent art collections which are open to the public. For example, Oxford possesses the imposing Ashmolean Museum of Art and Archaeology, Cambridge has the Fitzwilliam Museum and Birmingham has the Barber Institute. Staff and student art clubs often arrange one-man shows in addition to the exhibitions which are sponsored by the university.

The universities have found that an effective way of encouraging interest in the arts and, at the same time, providing financial help to a young painter or sculptor is by the establishment of 'creative' fellowships. The holder – an artist, sculptor, musician, poet or dramatist – receives a modest stipend and working facilities to paint or to write. For example, Nottingham has a Fellowship in Painting, and creative fellowships exist at Leeds, Bristol, Keele and York. Where the fellowship is held by a painter or sculptor he is usually given a chance to exhibit his work.

Some universities, such as Oxford and Cambridge, have a long theatrical tradition. The Amateur Dramatic Club at Cambridge was founded in 1855 and its theatre is a fully licensed public theatre. The policy is to present a student play every week of term and to provide a home for town amateur groups in vacations. ADC productions are reviewed in the national newspapers and all productions are widely advertised in Cambridge as well as in the university.

Oxford has had a Playhouse since 1923 and its purpose is to provide 'a permanent home for both a resident professional company and the amateur dramatic societies of Town and Gown'. Productions are open to the public and are widely advertised. Performances are presented by the Oxford University Dramatic Society and the University Opera Club. Repertory is provided by a professional company. Manchester, Southampton, Exeter, Edinburgh are among the universities which have opened their own theatres in recent years. Several other universities have ambitious plans for theatre building. Generally, the universities are anxious that the general public should attend drama productions. During vacations university theatres depend on public patronage and during these periods the productions are often presented by 'town' amateur societies as well as by professional companies.

57 In 1966 the Oxford University Dramatic Society put on a production of Marlowe's *Dr Faustus*. In this scene Richard Burton appears as Dr Faustus with an Oxford student, Andreas Teuber, playing the monk. Elizabeth Taylor also appeared in the play.

Musical activities vary from one university to another but it is often possible for a member of the public to listen to a varied selection of music at his local university. At some universities he can enjoy performances by outstanding soloists and chamber ensembles. He can also attend concerts given by amateurs and less well-known professionals; and he may be able to join the music society, orchestra and choir.

A further field of university 'extension' activity is the contribution made to adult education programmes on radio and television. The programmes with which universities are associated can be divided into three main types, namely, general knowledge, basic teaching and refresher courses. General knowledge programmes deal with a subject quite briefly and aim to arouse and widen the interests of viewers or listeners. The aim of a basic teaching programme is to present the elementary principles of a subject, such as economics. Refresher courses cover a wide field and have included a series for teachers of mathematics in primary schools; a course on industrial relations; and programmes for medical practitioners.

The major advantage of educational broadcasting is that it enables distinguished scholars who are also excellent lecturers to communicate with a far larger number of people than would otherwise be possible. One university – the Open University – relies to a great extent on television and radio broadcasting to provide tuition for its students. The Open University is described in Chapter 9.

Publishing is another service activity undertaken by the universities. Eight universities (Cambridge, Leicester, Liverpool, London, Manchester, Oxford, Edinburgh and Wales) have their own Press while many others arrange for or

58 Machinery at the Oxford University Press, 1888.

subsidise the publication of books by commercial publishers. Cambridge was empowered to print in 1534 by Henry VIII and 52 years later Oxford received the same privilege. Both the Oxford and Cambridge Presses enjoy a special position as publishers of the Authorized Version of the Bible. The other Presses are a development of the twentieth century.

Generally, university Presses form part of the university and are governed by a committee made up of members of the Senate. They do not confine their publications to the work of authors within their own university. It is the policy of most Presses to include a wide range of subjects and the Oxford University Press, for example, is one of the largest general publishers in the world. The university Presses exist primarily to publish worthwhile books with such a limited appeal that they could not be published at a profit. Commercial publishers are willing to include a certain number of such books in their lists, but they cannot be expected to do this on any scale. Thus universities play a vital and useful role in the world of publishing.

FURTHER READING

Joyce Long, *Universities and the General Public* University of Birmingham
J. H. Newman, *The Idea of a University* Longmans

9 The Future of the University

This chapter outlines three recent developments in university education. These are the establishment of the Open University; the development of a 'university role' by the polytechnics; and the move to establish an Independent University.

The Open University

The number of universities in the United Kingdom increased dramatically during the 1960s. (See Chapter 5). There are, however, many thousands of people of ability who are unable through circumstances to benefit from this growth. These people are the adults who have full-time responsibilities at work or at home and who cannot take three or four years off to study at a university. It was primarily to meet this situation that the Open University was founded in 1969.

Why the 'Open' University?

The title was chosen to demonstrate that the new University is 'Open' to people, to places and to new teaching methods.

Unlike other universities, the Open University does not lay down any particular academic qualifications for entry. Anyone may apply for admission provided they are over 21 years of age at the start of the course and are resident in the United Kingdom. Failure at one stage of a course is the only barrier to entering the next stage. Thus Open University students differ from other undergraduates in that they are not required to have GCE Advanced or Ordinary level passes for entry; they are usually over 21 and in full-time employment; they study mainly at home and in their spare time.

The University is also 'Open' as to places. Students live in every part of the United Kingdom. The teaching system brings the University to a student in his or her own home, and to local centres located throughout the country. For this purpose 12 regions have been set up, each headed by a Regional Director. The regional organisation provides the basis of the personal tutorial services to students and the framework of their corporate life as undergraduates.

Students at conventional universities live and study within a small area and this arrangement makes for considerable social and cultural contact. Students at the Open University are spread throughout the country and so miss this daily contact with fellow students. Recognising that this can be a disadvantage, the University has taken certain steps to minimise it. They include plans for a monthly student newspaper, a weekly radio news programme and a monthly television programme. In addition, as will be described later, there is the opportunity to meet others at local study centres and summer schools. The wearing of University ties, badges and scarves also encourages contact between students to some extent.

59 Map of the British Isles showing the twelve regions of the Open University.

The fact that students would live in every part of the United Kingdom meant that the Open University was faced with the challenge of using modern long-distance communications to bring higher education into the home. In this respect the University was 'Open' as to methods of teaching. Tuition is provided through the use of various methods of communication.

At regular intervals throughout their course students receive specially written correspondence packages. In addition to written material, the packages may also include slides, films, records or kits for home experiments. Most packages contain an assignment requiring written work to be submitted by a student. This is sent, via the University, to a course tutor for marking. The student is then advised on the progress he is making. Marks attained in each assignment are recorded and used as part of the final assessment of a student's performance.

Open University programmes are broadcast weekly on BBC television and radio. Broadcasts do not merely repeat material in the correspondence texts. Sometimes the author of the text explains part of the work in more detail. Other programmes bring eminent scholars, often from other universities, into the radio or television studio.

Study centres are used to provide facilities for watching and listening to programmes, for group discussion and for personal interviews with counsellors. These

60 Over 100 items of scientific apparatus are included in the home experimental kit which is sent to all students of the science foundation course of the Open University. The kit is designed to give all students laboratory experience within their own home.

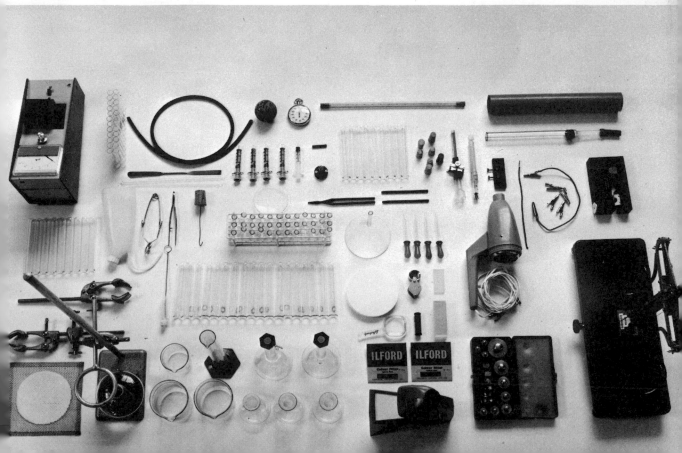

61 An interview for an Open University case study programme being recorded in Brazil with Dr. de Mendonca, Director of the Space Research Centre, Brazil. The Open Universities unique exploitation of modern communications enables it to provide students with a wide range of source material for their courses.

centres comprise rooms in a local school or college and are usually open each weekday evening from 6.30 p.m. to about 9 p.m. and in some cases at certain times during the weekend.

Residential summer schools are held to provide students with an intensive period of study. A summer school lasting one week is compulsory for every first-year student. The schools are held in the buildings of a number of universities during July, August and September.

Thus tuition extends over the length and breadth of the country to reach an annual student intake equal to almost half that of all other British universities put together. Each student is assigned to a counsellor whose job it is to guide and advise him in his studies. The counsellor meets students in local study centres, holds discussion groups and gives advice on general study problems. One of the specific jobs of the counsellor is to see students towards the end of their immediate course of study to discuss the subsequent courses they might follow. Course tutors who mark the correspondence work also hold tutorial classes in selected study centres.

These classes provide specialist academic tuition related to the current broadcast programmes and correspondence work.

In addition to their uses mentioned above, the network of study centres provides the basis for student participation in the University's policy-making. The University is aware of the maturity and wide collective experience of its students and it draws upon this in the development of policies in two ways. First, consultative committees at the study centres, and also at regional and national level, provide for regular consultation between staff and students. Secondly, there is a more formal Regional Assembly which provides a forum of discussion between the regional staff and students. Each Regional Assembly elects student and staff representatives to the General Assembly of the University. The General Assembly is entitled to express opinions to the Senate (which is responsible for the academic work of the University) on any matter affecting the work and interest of the University. A number of students are also elected to the Council, which is the executive governing body of the University.

62 A residential summer school provides science foundation course students of the Open University with an opportunity to undertake intensive practical laboratory work.

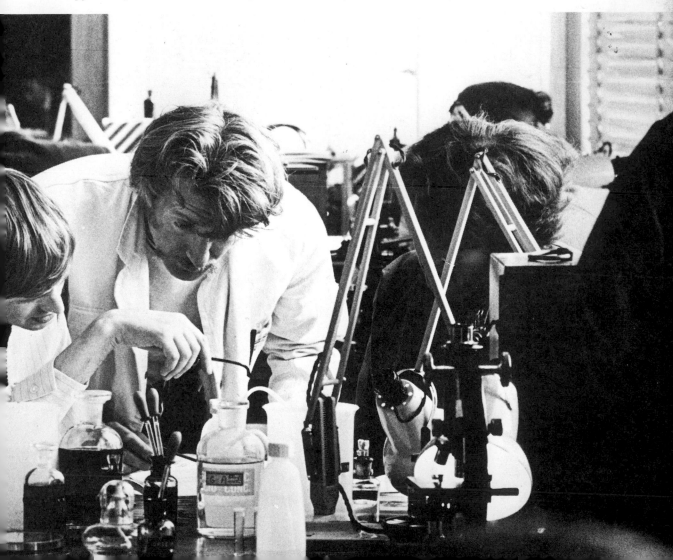

The programme of studies offered by the Open University differs from that of many traditional universities. Students are not confined to studies in only one or two subjects. There are six faculties – Arts, Educational Studies, Mathematics, Science, Social Science and Technology – and students may choose courses from more than one faculty.

The flexibility of the courses would have been impossible if several degrees, all with different regulations, had been introduced. For this reason the University decided to offer only one degree for undergraduates. All undergraduate degree programmes including those in science and technology lead to the degree of Bachelor of Arts (B.A.) either with or without honours. The B.A. degree is awarded to a student who obtains six course credits. The B.A. (Honours) degree is awarded for an additional two course credits, that is, a total of eight course credits.

63 Open University students taking the foundation course in arts discuss an aspect of the course.

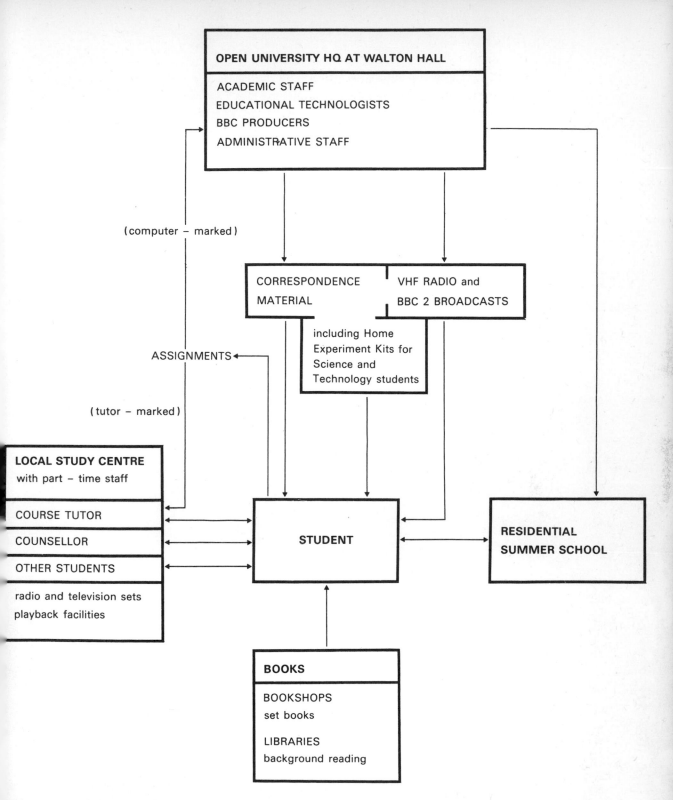

OPEN UNIVERSITY HQ AT WALTON HALL

ACADEMIC STAFF
EDUCATIONAL TECHNOLOGISTS
BBC PRODUCERS
ADMINISTRATIVE STAFF

(computer – marked)

CORRESPONDENCE
MATERIAL

VHF RADIO and
BBC 2 BROADCASTS

including Home
Experiment Kits for
Science and
Technology students

ASSIGNMENTS

(tutor – marked)

LOCAL STUDY CENTRE
with part – time staff

COURSE TUTOR

COUNSELLOR

OTHER STUDENTS

radio and television sets
playback facilities

STUDENT

**RESIDENTIAL
SUMMER SCHOOL**

BOOKS

BOOKSHOPS
set books

LIBRARIES
background reading

64 The organisation of studies at the Open University.

The successful completion of a one-year course leads to the award of a credit. Each credit is awarded on the basis of a student's best correspondence assignments and an examination. Normally students are not allowed to register for more than two courses in any one academic year. Thus the minimum time required for obtaining a degree is usually three years, and for the B.A. (Honours) degree, four years. Course credits can be accumulated over any number of years beyond the minimum. Certain educational requirements such as a recognised teaching certificate, may give an undergraduate up to three credit exemptions which will count towards the total credits needed for a degree. Thus existing achievements in higher education can be used as stepping-stones towards full degree status.

The University plans to offer courses leading to higher degrees to those who are already graduates. Like the first degree, these higher degrees will be obtained by part-time study and by the acquisition of a number of credits. The higher degrees are Bachelor of Philosophy (B.Phil.), Master of Philosophy (M.Phil.) and Doctor of Philosophy (Ph.D.). In addition to providing for non-residential students studying for higher degrees, facilities are available at the headquarters of the University – Milton Keynes in north Buckinghamshire – for a small number of residential students.

There are plans to award higher doctorates, namely, the Doctor of Letters (D.Litt.) and the Doctor of Science (D.Sc.). These degrees will be open only to graduates of the Open University and to members of the full-time staff.

From 1973 the Open University is providing a number of shorter Post-Experience Courses specially designed for people with experience of working in a special field who wish to extend their knowledge in that area. These courses vary in length and lead to a Certificate of Course Completion.

Over 42,000 men and women throughout the country applied to be registered as students for the Open University's first academic year beginning 1 January 1971. The number of applications received meant that many had to be disappointed – a situation determined by limited money, staff and space. Thus about 24,000 students started the first courses in January 1971. The number who sat the first examinations in October 1971 had fallen to 15,823, a reduction resulting from 'drop outs' from the course and failure to sit the examinations. Of this number 75 per cent gained credits – a result described by the Vice-Chancellor, Dr Walter Perry as 'a staggeringly high success rate'. He had not expected more than a 50 per cent pass.

There is a possibility that in 1973 the Government will introduce an experimental scheme to admit a limited number of 18-year olds to Open University degree courses.

The University Role of the Polytechnics

The thirty polytechnics have been formed from about seventy of the leading colleges of further education (the first three polytechnics were designated in January 1969). The formation of the polytechnics was designed to concentrate the full-time higher education work of the further education system at a limited number of strong centres. This policy was set out in a 1966 Government White Paper. The declared aim was to develop 'a distinctive sector of higher education within the further education system, to complement the universities and the colleges of education'.

The polytechnics cater for students of a wide range of ability and experience studying at many levels of higher education. There are full-time and sandwich course students working for degrees (including higher degrees) and for professional qualifications of degree standard or a little below degree standard. There are also students already in employment taking part-time courses leading to degrees and professional qualifications. Studies comprise the physical sciences, social sciences and the arts.

It is, however, with the 'university work' of the polytechnics that this section is concerned. For their degrees the polytechnics are dependent on the Council for National Academic Awards (CNAA). The Council, which was set up by Royal Charter in 1964, has powers to award first and higher degrees to students in establishments for Further Education outside the universities. Its Charter requires that the standard of these degrees should be comparable with that of university degrees. Such has been the pace of the CNAAs activities and the response of the colleges to the opportunities presented, that there are now some 24,000 students following CNAA courses in over seventy subjects.

The courses lead to the first degrees of B.A. and B.Sc.. More than half of the CNAA degree courses are 'sandwich' in character. This means a course consisting of periods of study in college combined with one or more stages of practical training in industry, commerce or professional work. The sandwich course lasts about four years compared with the three years usually spent on a full-time course. Compared with the London external degree course (where the control of examinations and syllabuses are largely out of the hands of the colleges), the CNAA degree course offers considerable advantages to colleges and students alike.

The colleges are allowed a wide measure of freedom to plan and develop their own courses. They can, therefore, reflect the needs of industry and commerce and the experience of teaching staffs. The colleges are also permitted to examine their own students with the help of external examiners approved by the Council.

At the same time, it should be emphasised that the Council does not approve a degree course submitted by a college until it has carried out a rigorous examination both of the proposed course and of facilities and accommodation at the college. Approval is given only if the high standard required by the Council is met.

The range of degree courses now offered under the auspices of the CNAA provides the first opportunity in this country for the award of a degree in certain subjects. Examples are the B.Sc. degrees in ceramics, textile marketing, information science, urban land economics, printing and photographic technology. The Council has also approved a number of inter-disciplinary courses such as chemistry with German or business administration, metallurgy and materials, languges and

65   A new type of course developed by the CNAA is the Combined Honours degree, in which students study two related subjects. This girl is taking French and biology.

economics. These courses are aimed at producing more graduates able to meet the new demands facing industry. Such topics are scarcely touched upon in the universities and the CNAA courses are far more vocationally biased than the great majority of university courses. Thus CNAA courses are a genuine alternative for students who want to take a vocationally-orientated degree.

Apart from the nature of the course offered, in what other ways do the polytechnics differ from the universities?

Firstly, polytechnics do not receive finance from the University Grants Committee; secondly, their work is not limited almost exclusively to degree studies and to full-time students; thirdly, they have not received Royal Charters to award their own degrees; fourthly, their senior academic posts are not defined as that of 'professor'.

In addition to CNAA degrees many polytechnics (and technical colleges) offer full-time courses for London external degrees.

The Independent University

The Independent University was first advocated in a letter to the *Times* in May, 1967. It was envisaged as a university free from State support and dependent for finance primarily on the fees paid by its students. The purpose of the enterprise was to protect academic freedom from economic, governmental and student pressures. The response was immediate and the support was extensive.

With the aid of organisations like the Institute of Economic Affairs, the Independent University has progressed to a planning board, a permanent secretariat, a site in Buckinghamshire, and a 'shadow' vice-chancellor. There are, however, a number of political and social uncertainties that surround it and its future is unsettled.

FURTHER READING
Open University Guide for Applicants
University Independence, The Main Questions Editor: J. H. MacCullam Scott;
　Rex Collins
E. Robinson, *The New Polytechnics* Cornmarket

Index

Numbers in **bold type** refer to the figure numbers of the illustrations.

95